ANNIE RIGG is the author of over 15 cookbooks including *Eat More Veg*, the companion to this book. She is a Leith's-trained chef, has worked for Delia Smith, and is part of the *Great British Bake Off* team, recipe testing and writing some of the official GBBO guides.

EAT
MORE
VEGAN

WHEN USING KITCHEN APPLIANCES PLEASE ALWAYS FOLLOW THE
MANUFACTURER'S INSTRUCTIONS

Pavilion
An imprint of HarperCollins*Publishers* Ltd
1 London Bridge Street
London SE1 9GF

www.harpercollins.co.uk

HarperCollins*Publishers*
1st Floor, Watermarque Building, Ringsend Road
Dublin 4, Ireland

First published in Great Britain by Pavilion
An imprint of HarperCollins*Publishers* 2023

10 9 8 7 6 5 4 3 2 1

A catalogue record of this book is available from the British Library

ISBN 978-1-911-68251-6

Photographer: Nassima Rothacker
Design manager: Laura Russell
Designer: Kei Ishimaru
Commissioning editor: Lucy Smith
Managing editor: Clare Double
Home economist: Annie Rigg
Prop stylist: Jenny Ing
Food assistants: Lola Milne and Sarah Vassallo

Printed and bound in China

This book is produced from independently certified FSC™ paper to ensure
responsible forest management.

For more information visit: www.harpercollins.co.uk/green

EAT MORE
VEGAN

80 DELICIOUS RECIPES
EVERYONE WILL LOVE

ANNIE
RIGG

PAVILION

CONTENTS

INTRODUCTION

Eating vegan is a lifestyle change that many of us have already embraced, whether for ethical, environmental or health reasons. If you are new to vegan cooking you may well be in for a few surprises. My focus throughout this book is on using vegetables, pulses, grains and seeds rather than meat replacements. All the recipes are for savoury dishes that are entirely vegan, including quick suppers and light bites, sides and salads, and everyday mains as well as more elaborate feasts that lend themselves to entertaining or weekend cooking.

For any cook, flavour, colour and texture are key to keeping our meals interesting and appetising – perhaps even more so when you follow a plant-based diet. All my dishes are visually appealing, tasty and a celebration of the wonderfully diverse selection of fresh, seasonal produce.

A well-stocked store cupboard is essential for most styles of cooking, particularly when preparing vegan meals. Some of the recipes in the book have fairly long lists of ingredients, but often these are spices or other store-cupboard items. A selection of seeds and ground spices is vital, as are – for me, at least – chillies in umpteen forms and levels of heat: dried flakes, fine powders, hot oils and sauces are among my go-to seasonings. Packs of dried lentils, beans and peas and either cans or jars of good-quality, ready-to-use pulses are an important source of protein for a vegan diet. Weight for weight, dried pulses are often far cheaper than tinned; they take up less space and are available in a wider range. It's well worth seeking out local producers of exceptional pulses, all of which are now easily available online.

Plenty of my recipes take inspiration from classic Indian and Southeast Asian dishes, many of them vegetarian and which, with a few judicious swaps or subs, can easily become vegan. Dahl, for instance, can be made with different pulses for a quick, nutritious supper. I like to serve dahl with a side of rice, pickles and flatbread. Tofu, a staple of East Asian cuisine, is a brilliant vegan stand-in for paneer cheese; it makes a wonderful creamy Caesar salad dressing, a tasty filling for Greek-style filo pastries and, because it absorbs flavours so well, it is the ideal vehicle for the punchiest of hot chilli sauces. Vegan Thai fish sauce is a fairly new ingredient to hit our shelves. It imparts some of the flavour profile of the original fish sauce (without the fish!) that is crucial to Thai-style salads and soups.

Equipped with a choice of rice, pasta and other grains in your cupboard you're never more than minutes away from dinner. I prefer brown rice over white rice as a side and I find freekeh, pearl barley and spelt terrific in salads, stews, soups and salads.

An array of oils, both for cooking and dressing finished dishes, is welcome, too. Aside from the familiar — sunflower, extra virgin olive and coconut oil — having a good-quality toasted sesame oil for finishing rice or noodle dishes is key, while a drizzle of avocado, pumpkin seed, hazelnut, walnut or argan oil over salads can really enhance their flavour. Jars of tahini (sesame seed paste), for Middle Eastern dishes, and miso (fermented soya bean paste), for Japanese recipes, are two more store-cupboard items I wouldn't be without — they add a depth of flavour to soups, stews and dressings. On the subject of flavour bombs, another handy ingredient that features in many of my recipes is nutritional yeast. This is dried deactivated yeast, which may not sound particularly appealing, but it adds an almost cheese-like flavour to many vegan sauces, gratins, pasta dishes and bakes.

And now the spotlight is turned on the incredible range of veggies! The variety of fresh, seasonal produce is fabulous and exciting. Each season brings a wealth of new and more varied vegetables — from the glory of asparagus, spinach and radishes in spring, the multi-coloured boxes of tomatoes and salad leaves of summer, to the luscious brassicas and greens of autumn and heritage root veg of winter. Check out your local farmers' markets and greengrocers as well as supermarkets and online suppliers.

If you are lucky enough to have your own garden, you will understand the joy of being able to grow your own veg. For flavour and freshness nothing beats digging potatoes from the soil, snipping tomatoes off the vine or podding your own peas. Even if you don't have a garden with raised beds, you can still grow tomatoes and lettuces in tubs or herbs in pots on windowsills or in window boxes. Basil, chives, oregano, thyme and rosemary are the herbs I grow within easy reach outside my back door during summer. Woody sage and bay need regular haircuts to keep them in check, but as their leaves are used so frequently it's never a problem.

Whether you are already opting for a plant-based diet or wanting to eat vegan for a few days each week, my hope is that this book will inspire your cooking and encourage you to explore and enjoy more vegan meals. It's the way forward....

QUICK SUPPERS

COURGETTE SPAGHETTI WITH PEA 'PESTO'

This delicious supper dish can be prepared in the time it takes to bring a pan of water to boil and cook some pasta — and that's a winner on many levels in my house. You can also prepare the pea pesto in advance and keep it in the fridge for 24 hours until ready to cook. Frozen peas work brilliantly in this pesto as they cook so quickly; if you are using fresh peas they will take a few minutes longer to cook until tender.

SERVES 4

350g dried spaghetti
   or linguine
3 courgettes
2 tbsp olive oil
1 fat garlic clove, crushed
2 tsp fresh thyme leaves
Vegan Italian-style cheese,
   nutritional yeast or
   Pangrattato (see page 155),
   to serve

PESTO

100g garden peas, fresh
   or frozen
1 fat garlic clove, crushed
4 tbsp extra virgin olive oil
2 tsp lemon juice
30g pine kernels, toasted
2 tsp nutritional yeast
2 tbsp roughly chopped
   basil leaves
1 tbsp roughly chopped
   flat-leaf parsley
Salt and freshly ground
   black pepper

Bring a large pan of water to the boil and add 2 tsp salt.

Meanwhile, make the pesto. Blanch the peas for 1 minute if using frozen and 2 minutes if fresh, then remove from the pan with a slotted spoon and refresh under cold running water. Drain well and tip into the bowl of a food processor. Add 1 clove crushed garlic, the extra virgin olive oil, lemon juice, toasted pine kernels, nutritional yeast, chopped basil and flat-leaf parsley. Season well with salt and freshly ground black pepper and whizz until combined and nearly smooth. Set aside until ready to serve.

Cook the pasta in the boiling water following the packet instructions.

Meanwhile, prepare the courgettes. Use a julienne grater to cut the courgettes into long, spaghetti-thin strips. Heat the olive oil in a large frying pan over a medium heat, add the crushed garlic and the thyme and cook for 30 seconds before adding the courgette strips. Cook quickly for a further 30 seconds to 1 minute, stirring constantly, until just starting to soften. Slide the pan off the heat until the pasta is cooked.

Reserving 1 cup of the cooking water, drain the pasta and add it to the courgettes with all but 1 tbsp of the pea pesto. Mix well to combine over a medium–high heat. Add a little pasta cooking water to loosen the spaghetti strands. Season and divide between bowls. Top each bowl with a small spoonful of pea pesto and serve with vegan Italian-style cheese, a little nutritional yeast or pangrattato scattered over the top.

TERIYAKI AUBERGINE AND KING OYSTER MUSHROOMS
WITH SESAME RICE

For this recipe you will need to make teriyaki sauce, which takes a matter of moments – you can use store-bought, but homemade is best and probably less sugared than most commercially produced sauces. 'Teriyaki' refers to the cooking method and roughly translates as 'glazed and grilled'. The side of pickled ginger is entirely optional and the kimchi is far from in keeping with the Japanese theme – but either works well to cut through the salty, slightly sweet teriyaki sauce.

SERVES 2

1 large aubergine
2 king oyster mushrooms
180g sushi rice
150g purple sprouting or
    tenderstem broccoli
2 tsp toasted sesame seeds,
    plus extra to serve
2 tsp toasted sesame oil
1 spring onion, finely sliced
1 tbsp pickled ginger or
    kimchi (optional)

TERIYAKI SAUCE

5 tbsp soy sauce
4 tbsp mirin
2 tbsp sake
1 tbsp rice vinegar
1 tbsp soft brown or golden
    caster sugar
1 garlic clove, crushed
1 tsp grated fresh ginger

Start by making the teriyaki sauce. Combine all the ingredients in a small pan and bring to the boil over a low–medium heat. Simmer for 1 minute and then remove from the heat and leave to cool slightly.

Cut the aubergine and king oyster mushrooms into 1cm-thick slices and arrange in a single layer on a tray. Spoon over half the teriyaki sauce, turn to coat the veggies in the sauce and set aside to marinate for 30 minutes, turning the veggies again halfway through.

Meanwhile, wash the sushi rice and soak in cold water for 30 minutes.

Drain the rice, tip into a small saucepan and cover with about 300ml cold water and add a pinch of salt. Bring to the boil, half-cover the pan with a lid and simmer for about 10 minutes or until almost all the water has evaporated. Remove from the heat, cover the pan and set aside to steam the rice while you cook the veggies.

Heat a griddle pan over a medium–high heat. Add the marinated aubergine and mushroom slices, brush with the remaining teriyaki sauce and cook, turning frequently, until tender and nicely browned.

In a separate pan steam the broccoli until tender. Stir the toasted sesame seeds and sesame oil into the rice and divide between two bowls. Top with the teriyaki aubergine and mushrooms, scatter with more sesame seeds and sliced spring onions and serve with the steamed broccoli and a side of pickled ginger or kimchi, if you like.

KUKU SABZI

Kuku Sabzi is a Persian herb frittata which has a vast ratio of herbs to eggs. In this recipe I add chard or cavolo nero to the herb mixture to up the veggie content and use gram flour and plant-based Greek-style yogurt in place of eggs.

SERVES 4

1 tsp coriander seeds
1 tsp cumin seeds
1 leek
1 onion
3 tbsp olive oil
2 garlic cloves, crushed
1 tsp ground turmeric
½ tsp cayenne pepper
100g rainbow chard or
  cavolo nero, washed
1 small bunch of dill
1 small bunch of
  flat-leaf parsley
1 small bunch of coriander
50g walnuts, roughly
  chopped
75g gram flour
2 tbsp vegan Greek-style
  yogurt
1 tsp nutritional yeast
  (optional)
Juice of ½ lemon
Salt and freshly ground
  black pepper

Preheat the oven to 170°C fan/190°C/gas mark 5.

Tip the coriander and cumin seeds into a medium (20cm) non-stick oven-proof sauté or frying pan and toast over a medium heat for about 1 minute or until fragrant. Coarsely grind the toasted spices using a pestle and mortar (or the end of a rolling pin and a small bowl).

Trim and cut the leek into 5mm-thick rounds and slice the onion. Heat 2 tbsp of the olive oil in the frying pan over a medium heat. Add the sliced leek and onion and cook, stirring frequently, for about 10 minutes until soft and just starting to brown at the edges. Add the coriander and cumin seeds, crushed garlic, turmeric and cayenne, mix well and cook for a further minute.

Cut the chard or cavolo nero into ribbons, add to the pan and cook for about 2 minutes, stirring, until wilted. Tip the contents of the pan into a bowl and leave to cool slightly while you prepare the remaining ingredients – no need to wash the pan as you'll need it again.

Chop the herbs (leaves and stalks) and add to the cooled leek mixture with the chopped walnuts. In another bowl whisk together the gram flour, yogurt, nutritional yeast (if using), lemon juice and 100ml water. Season well with salt and freshly ground black pepper and whisk again. Add to the leek mixture and stir to combine.

Heat another tablespoon of olive oil in the frying pan over a medium heat, add the kuku sabzi mixture and cook, without stirring, for about 2 minutes until the edges and underside are starting to turn golden. Transfer the pan to the oven and cook for a further 20 minutes until set.

Loosen the edges of the kuku sabzi with a palette knife, turn out of the pan onto a board and leave to cool to room temperature before cutting into slices to serve.

TOMATOEY BEANS WITH CAVOLO NERO

Posh beans on toast… Serve them on chargrilled sourdough or focaccia or with a salad of peppery leaves, such as rocket. The beans can be eaten hot, warm or at room temperature and will reheat beautifully. The cavolo nero can be swapped for spring greens, rainbow chard, spinach, thinly sliced courgettes or even a large handful of basil leaves. Try serving with a good dollop of aioli in place of the balsamic and olive oil.

SERVES 2 GENEROUSLY

1 onion, sliced
2 tbsp extra virgin olive oil,
   plus extra for drizzling
2 garlic cloves, thinly sliced
4 tomatoes, halved
8 cherry tomatoes
1 x 400g can of butter beans,
   drained and rinsed
250ml vegetable stock
1 sprig of rosemary
1 bay leaf
1 pared strip of lemon zest
50g trimmed cavolo nero,
   rinsed and sliced into
   ribbons
Salt and freshly ground
   black pepper

TO SERVE

2 thick slices sourdough
   bread or focaccia
1 garlic clove, cut in half
Balsamic vinegar, to drizzle

Preheat the oven to 160°C fan/180°C/gas mark 4.

Tip the onion into an ovenproof sauté pan, add 1 tbsp of the olive oil and cook over a medium heat, stirring frequently, for about 8 minutes until softened and starting to turn golden brown at the edges.

Add the garlic to the pan and continue to cook for a further minute. Add all the tomatoes, together with the drained butter beans. Season well with salt and freshly ground black pepper and pour over the vegetable stock. Add the leaves from the rosemary sprig, the bay leaf and lemon zest and bring to the boil.

Drizzle with the remaining olive oil, cover either with a lid or a disc of baking paper and cook in the oven for about 30 minutes, until the tomatoes are soft and very juicy and break up when stirred.

Remove the lemon zest from the beans, stir in the cavolo nero, cover and cook for a further 5 minutes until the greens are soft and wilted.

Meanwhile, toast the bread either under the grill or on a ridged griddle pan and rub with the cut side of the garlic clove. Spoon the beans on top of the bread, drizzle with balsamic vinegar and olive oil and serve.

PALAK 'PANEER'

Palak is Hindi for spinach, and paneer is a firm cow's milk cheese that is very similar to extra firm tofu in texture and flavour, so tofu makes a wonderful alternative in this dish. Marinating the tofu for at least 1 hour before cooking gives it an extra savoury note. Be sure to use young tender leaf spinach for this dish and don't worry about trimming the stalks – it can all go in. Serve Palak Paneer with Quick Flatbreads (see page 158) and assorted Indian pickles.

SERVES 4

250g extra firm tofu
Juice of ½ lemon
1 tsp nutritional yeast
½ tsp garam masala
350g young spinach, washed
1 large green chilli, roughly
    chopped (include the seeds
    if you like extra heat)
2 fat garlic cloves, crushed
3 tsp grated fresh ginger
2 tbsp coconut oil
1 onion, finely chopped
1 large tomato, chopped
½ tsp fenugreek seeds
½ tsp cumin seed
¼ tsp cayenne pepper
1 tbsp sunflower oil
4–5 tbsp coconut milk,
    cashew cream or coyo
    (coconut milk yogurt)
Salt and freshly ground
    black pepper

Start by marinating the tofu. Pat the tofu dry on kitchen paper and cut into 1–2cm dice. Tip into a bowl, add the lemon juice, nutritional yeast and a good pinch of garam masala. Mix well to combine, cover and set aside for 1 hour.

Meanwhile, blanch the spinach in boiling water or steam it until just wilted. Drain through a colander and refresh under cold running water. Squeeze dry and tip the spinach into a blender. Add the green chilli to the blender with half the garlic and half the ginger. Season with salt and freshly ground black pepper, blend until nearly smooth and set aside.

Heat the coconut oil in a wok or sauté pan, add the onion and cook over a medium heat, stirring from time to time, for about 10 minutes, until soft but not coloured. Add the remaining garlic and ginger, the chopped tomato and spices. Season with salt and freshly ground black pepper and continue to cook for a further 5 minutes over a low–medium heat until the tomato has cooked and thickened.

While the onion mixture is cooking heat 1 tbsp sunflower oil in a frying pan over a medium–high heat, drain the tofu from the marinade, add to the pan and fry quickly until golden brown on all sides.

Add the spinach purée and 150ml water to the onions, mix well and cook for 2 minutes, adding a little more water if needed to make the mixture a sauce rather than a thick purée. Add the tofu, 3 tbsp of the coconut milk and another good pinch of garam masala. Mix well and cook for a further minute before serving drizzled with more coconut milk. Be careful not to overcook the spinach – it should still be a vibrant green.

DAN DAN NOODLES

This recipe is not an authentic interpretation of the popular Sichuan street food Dan Dan noodles — that uses minced pork in the sauce — but it is a very tasty plant-based alternative that can be cooked in the time it takes to boil a pan of water and cook the noodles. Egg noodles would usually be the noodle of choice here, but either wheat udon or ramen are a fine alternative. Traditionally, Dan Dan noodles will include Chinese pickled mustard greens, which are available in Chinese supermarkets or online. If you can find them, do add a tablespoonful to the sauce. If you prefer, you could use tahini in the sauce instead of peanut butter.

SERVES 4

270g dried udon noodles
15g dried sliced shiitake mushrooms
2 tbsp sunflower or rapeseed oil
2 fat garlic cloves, crushed
2 tsp grated fresh ginger
1 red chilli, finely chopped
1 tsp Sichuan peppercorns, lightly crushed
150g chestnut or shiitake mushrooms
4 spring onions, white and green parts separated
125g firm tofu
200g choy sum

Bring a large pan of salted water to the boil for the noodles. Tip the dried shiitake mushrooms into a small bowl, cover with 100ml just-boiled water and leave to soak for about 5 minutes while you prepare the remaining ingredients.

Heat the oil in a large frying pan or wok over a medium heat and add the garlic, ginger and chilli. Cook for 2–3 minutes, stirring frequently, until soft but not coloured. Add the Sichuan peppercorns and cook for a further minute until aromatic.

Trim and finely chop the chestnut mushrooms. Finely slice the white parts of the spring onions (shred and reserve the green parts for garnish), drain and finely chop the tofu. Drain the rehydrated shiitake mushrooms through a sieve into a bowl, reserving the soaking liquid. Add them, along with the chestnut mushrooms, spring onion whites and tofu, to the pan and continue to cook for a further 4–5 minutes, stirring frequently, until the mushrooms are very tender.

Meanwhile, cook the noodles in the boiling water following the packet instructions and prepare the sauce. Add all the ingredients for the sauce to the mushroom soaking water and whisk together until combined.

SAUCE

2 tbsp unsweetened
   peanut butter
2 tbsp soy sauce
1 tbsp Chinkiang, rice or
   balsamic vinegar
1 tbsp toasted sesame oil
1 garlic clove, crushed
1 tsp grated fresh ginger
1 tsp Chinese five-spice
1 tsp soft light brown sugar
   or maple syrup

TO SERVE

3 tsp toasted sesame seeds
Chilli oil

Cut the choy sum into 1cm strips, separating the leafy parts from the stalks. Add the chopped stalks to the pan and cook for a minute until just softened, then add the shredded leaves and cook for a further 30 seconds until wilted. Pour in the sauce mixture, stir to combine and add a little of the noodle cooking water to loosen if the sauce seems too dry. Using tongs, drop the noodles straight into the pan and combine, adding more noodle water if needed to coat the noodles in sauce.

Divide the noodles between bowls, scatter with the reserved shredded spring onion greens and sesame seeds, and serve with chilli oil.

'SUSHI' BOWLS

These bowls have all the elements of vegan sushi rolls minus the seaweed — you can always include some crisped and shredded nori if you like but there is already quite a rainbow in each bowl. The vegetables can be swapped depending on what you prefer, but include a variety of textures and colours. The tofu is baked and therefore uses less oil than if you were to fry it, but if you'd rather not put the oven on, just fry the marinated tofu in a little sunflower oil in a non-stick pan.

SERVES 4

200g extra firm tofu
1 garlic clove, grated
2 tsp grated fresh ginger
4 tbsp soy sauce
2 tbsp chilli sauce
2 tbsp maple or agave syrup
4 tsp sesame oil
4 tsp sesame seeds, plus
   extra to serve
1 tbsp cornflour
200g brown jasmine rice
8 radishes, trimmed and
   thinly sliced
16 sugar snaps, halved
1 avocado, stoned, peeled
   and sliced
4 tbsp podded edamame
   beans
1 carrot, julienned
¼ unpeeled cucumber,
   julienned
A handful of baby leaf
   spinach or fiery leaves
   such as mizuna or wasabi
1 tbsp rice vinegar
Pickled ginger (optional),
   to serve

Pat the tofu dry on a double thickness of kitchen paper and cut into 1cm slices or dice. In a large bowl combine the garlic, ginger, 2 tbsp soy sauce, 1 tbsp chilli sauce, 1 tbsp maple syrup, 2 tsp sesame oil and 2 tsp sesame seeds. Add the tofu and mix to coat thoroughly. Cover and set aside to marinate for 30 minutes.

Preheat the oven to 170°C fan/190°C/gas mark 5 and line a baking tray with baking parchment.

Sprinkle the cornflour over the marinated tofu and mix to combine. Arrange on the lined baking tray in a single layer and bake for about 30 minutes, turning halfway through, until crisp and golden brown.

Meanwhile, cook the rice in boiling salted water following the packet instructions. Drain, leave to cool and divide between 4 serving bowls.

Divide the prepared veggies between the bowls and tuck in the baby spinach or salad leaves. Combine the rice vinegar with the remaining soy sauce, chilli sauce, maple syrup and sesame oil in a small bowl and drizzle over the salad bowls. Scatter with more sesame seeds and serve with a little pickled ginger on the side, if you like.

GREEN VEG STIR-FRY

This is what I eat when I don't want to spend hours in front of the cooker. Bright, crisp green veggies, cooked quickly to preserve their vibrancy and with varying amounts of garlic, ginger and chilli depending on my mood — which always means plenty of garlic, ginger and chilli… The vegetable combination can be adapted to the season and what you have in your fridge. The sweetness of Brussels sprouts pairs brilliantly with the aromatics. Shredded spring greens, peppers, beansprouts, courgettes and fine green beans are all perfect subs for any of the suggested ingredients. Steamed rice or noodles complete the meal. The quantities in this recipe serve 2 because that is what will comfortably fit in a regular-size wok, but they can be scaled up as needed.

SERVES 2

150g tenderstem or purple
   sprouting broccoli
6 asparagus spears
100g sugar snaps
3 baby pak choi
8 Brussels sprouts
¼ Chinese leaf
2 spring onions
1 fat garlic clove, crushed
1 mild red chilli, finely
   chopped
2 tsp grated fresh ginger
1–2 tbsp sunflower oil
1 tbsp soy sauce, plus extra
   to serve
2–3 tsp toasted sesame oil

TO SERVE

Steamed rice or noodles
2 tsp toasted sesame seeds
Chilli oil, kimchi or
   Furikake (see page 160)

Start by preparing all of the vegetables, which should be cut to a similar size to ensure that they all cook at the same time. Trim the broccoli and cut each stalk in half. Trim the asparagus and cut on the diagonal into bite-size pieces. Cut the sugar snaps and pak choi in half. Thickly shred the Brussels sprouts and Chinese leaf.

Shred the green parts of the spring onions for garnish, and reserve. Cut the white parts into slices and tip into a wok or large frying pan with the garlic, chilli and ginger. Add 1 tbsp sunflower oil and stir-fry over a medium heat for about 1 minute to cook out the raw flavours of the aromatics.

Add all the prepared veggies to the wok and continue to cook for a further 5 minutes, stirring almost constantly, until the vegetables are tender but still crisp. Add the soy sauce and sesame oil to the pan, stir quickly to combine and then spoon the veggies on top of cooked rice or noodles and scatter with toasted sesame seeds and the reserved spring onion tops.

Serve with extra soy sauce and chilli oil, kimchi and/or a good sprinkling of furikake.

SINGAPORE NOODLES

These super-tasty, super-quick noodles can be on the plate in under 15 minutes. As with all stir-fries, the key to quick cooking is to have all the ingredients prepared before you start. The veggie selection can vary depending on personal preference but should be brightly coloured, crisp and cut to the same size so that they all cook at the same time. Baby corn, fine green beans, peas, edamame or shiitake mushrooms would all be delicious additions or alternatives.

SERVES 2 GENEROUSLY OR 4 AS A LIGHT MEAL

175–200g rice vermicelli
  noodles
100g extra firm tofu
1 small onion, sliced
1 garlic clove, crushed
1 small red chilli, finely
  chopped
2cm piece fresh ginger,
  finely chopped
2 spring onions, sliced
1 small red pepper, deseeded
  and cut into strips
75g sugar snaps, halved
75g tenderstem broccoli, cut
  into 1–2cm pieces
1 small carrot, julienned
8 tinned water chestnuts,
  drained and cut into
  matchsticks
1 handful beansprouts,
  rinsed
2 tbsp soy sauce
1 tbsp Shaoxing rice wine
1 tbsp medium curry powder
½ tsp Chinese five-spice
1–2 tbsp sunflower oil
2 tsp toasted sesame oil,
  to serve

Start by soaking the noodles in a large bowl of freshly boiled water following the packet instructions – usually between 5 and 10 minutes.

Meanwhile, pat the tofu dry on kitchen paper and cut into dice or batons. Prepare the onion, garlic, chilli, ginger and all the vegetables.

Drain the noodles through a sieve. In a small bowl combine the soy sauce, rice wine, curry powder, five-spice and 2 tbsp water.

Now you are ready to start stir-frying. Heat 1 tbsp of the sunflower oil in a large wok over a medium heat. Add the tofu and stir-fry for about 2 minutes until golden brown. Remove from the pan with a slotted spoon and set aside.

Add a little more oil to the wok if needed, add the sliced onions and stir-fry for 2 minutes until starting to soften and brown at the edges. Add the garlic, chilli, ginger and spring onions and fry for a further minute. Add the pepper, sugar snaps, broccoli, carrot and water chestnuts and stir-fry for 2 minutes until tender. Return the tofu to the pan along with the beansprouts and mix.

Tip the drained noodles into the wok and stir into the veggies. Add the sauce mixture and stir-fry for another minute or so until the ingredients are thoroughly combined and piping hot. Drizzle with sesame oil and serve immediately.

SPLIT PEA DAHL — TWO WAYS

Serve either of these dahls with steamed rice and pickles for a comforting midweek supper or as part of a larger curry-themed feast. It's difficult to be accurate on timings and the amount of water needed to make split pea dahl as it will depend on the age and brand of the dried pulses, but the cooked peas should be very soft and retain some texture, and the dahl should not be dry.

SERVES 4

YELLOW SPLIT PEA DAHL WITH TOMATOES AND ROASTED SQUASH

175g yellow split peas, rinsed thoroughly under cold running water

1 garlic clove, finely sliced

3cm piece fresh ginger, peeled and shredded

½ tsp ground turmeric

1 bay leaf

1 small cinnamon stick

2 cardamom pods

400g peeled and deseeded squash or pumpkin, cut into large dice

1 tbsp sunflower oil

½ tsp cumin seeds, lightly crushed

½ tsp coriander seeds, lightly crushed

12 cherry tomatoes, halved

½ tsp crushed dried chilli

3 tbsp coconut milk

2 tbsp coriander leaves, to serve

Salt and freshly ground black pepper

continues overleaf

Whichever dahl you make, drain the split peas and tip into a medium saucepan. Add the garlic and ginger to the pan with the turmeric, bay leaf, cinnamon stick and cardamom pods. Pour over 500ml water and bring slowly to the boil, reduce the heat to a very gentle simmer, half cover the pan with a lid and cook, stirring often, until the peas are very soft and somewhat broken down (about 30 minutes). You may need to add more water if the peas require longer to soften and cook.

For the yellow split pea dahl, roast the squash and tomatoes while the dahl is cooking. Preheat the oven to 180°C fan/200°C/gas mark 6. Put the squash on a baking tray, coat in the sunflower oil, add the cumin and coriander seeds, season and roast for about 20 minutes, turning halfway through, until starting to soften. Add the cherry tomatoes, cut side up, and crushed dried chilli. Cook for a further 10 minutes until the squash is golden at the edges and the tomatoes have softened.

Remove the bay leaf, cinnamon stick and cardamom pods from the dahl. Add the roasted veggies and coconut milk, season well with salt and freshly ground black pepper and scatter with coriander leaves to serve.

continues overleaf

SERVES 4

GREEN SPLIT PEA DAHL WITH SPINACH AND BRUSSELS

175g green split peas, rinsed
   thoroughly under cold
   running water
1 garlic clove, finely sliced
3cm piece fresh ginger,
   peeled and shredded
½ tsp ground turmeric
1 bay leaf
1 small cinnamon stick
2 cardamom pods
100g young leaf spinach,
   washed
2 tbsp coriander leaves,
   to serve

BRUSSELS SPROUTS

1 tbsp coconut or
   sunflower oil
1 onion, sliced
1 garlic clove, crushed
2 tsp grated fresh ginger
1 tsp black mustard seeds
½ tsp crushed dried chilli
10 curry leaves
200g Brussels sprouts,
   trimmed and shredded

To make the green split pea dahl follow the instructions on page 26 for cooking the pulses until they are soft but not dry.

Meanwhile, prepare the Brussels sprout mixture. Heat the oil in a frying pan over medium heat. Add the onion and cook, stirring often, for about 10 minutes until the onion is soft and starting to turn golden at the edges. Add the garlic, ginger, mustard seeds, crushed dried chilli and curry leaves and cook for one minute. Add the sprouts and cook quickly until just tender.

Remove the bay leaf, cinnamon stick and cardamom pods from the dahl. Stir in the young spinach leaves and cook for a further minute until wilted, spoon into bowls and top with the onion and sprout mixture. Season well with salt and freshly ground black pepper and garnish with coriander leaves to serve.

TARRAGON MUSHROOMS ON TOAST WITH WILTED CHARD

A super-simple but deeply satisfying supper dish. Chestnut mushrooms have a good earthy flavour but feel free to add a handful of wild mushrooms or field mushrooms depending on the season and availability. Swap the tarragon for parsley or chives if you prefer.

SERVES 2

2 tbsp olive oil

400g chestnut mushrooms, trimmed and quartered

2 garlic cloves, crushed

2 thick slices of sourdough bread

200g rainbow chard, trimmed and cut into large bite-size pieces

A squeeze of lemon juice

3 heaped tbsp dairy-free crème fraîche

1 heaped tsp wholegrain mustard

1 tbsp roughly chopped tarragon

Salt and freshly ground black pepper

Heat 1 tbsp of the olive oil in a large frying pan over a high heat. Add the mushrooms, season and cook, stirring often, for 3–4 minutes until the mushrooms are tender and browned.

Add half the garlic and cook for a further minute.

Meanwhile, toast the sourdough on both sides.

Heat the remaining oil in another frying pan over a medium heat, add the rest of the garlic and cook for 30 seconds before adding the chard. Season and fry until just wilted. Add a squeeze of lemon juice, remove from the heat and set aside.

Add the crème fraîche, mustard and chopped tarragon to the garlicky mushrooms, mix well and cook for a further 30 seconds–1 minute to warm the crème fraîche.

Spoon the wilted chard onto the toasted sourdough, top with the creamy mushrooms and serve immediately.

MAINS

ONIGIRAZU (SUSHI SANDWICHES)

These sushi sandwiches are a fun and delicious lunch idea. Cook and chill the rice a few hours ahead so that it is sticky and easier to handle. The fillings are purely suggestions. You could swap the tofu for Teriyaki Aubergine (see page 15), sliced tomatoes, roasted peppers... the possibilities are endless. But, as with any sandwich, think about colour, flavour and texture. You want something crisp, something leafy and something pickled or spicy.

MAKES 4

200g sushi rice
2 tsp rice vinegar
1 tsp mirin
200g firm tofu
2 tbsp soy sauce, plus extra
   to serve
1 tbsp cornflour
2 tsp Korean chilli powder
1 tbsp sesame seeds
1 tbsp sunflower oil
10cm piece cucumber
4–6 radishes
1 avocado
1 cooked beetroot
1 carrot, peeled
4 sheets nori
4 tsp wasabi
A handful of baby
   spinach leaves
Pickled ginger
Mustard cress

Start by cooking the sushi rice following the packet instructions. Remove from the heat, dress with rice vinegar and mirin and leave to cool. Cover and chill until ready to assemble the onigirazu.

Cut the tofu into four 1cm-thick slices and dip into the soy sauce to coat on both sides. On a plate mix the cornflour, chilli powder and sesame seeds. Press each tofu slice into the mixture to coat on both sides. Heat the sunflower oil in a large frying pan over a medium–high heat. Fry the tofu for about 1 minute on each side until crisp and golden brown. Remove from the heat and leave to cool while you prepare the remaining ingredients.

Thinly slice the cucumber, radishes, avocado and beetroot and stack in neat separate piles. Cut the carrot into matchsticks.

Lay a sheet of clingfilm on the work surface and place one sheet of nori on top, shiny side down. Divide the cold rice into eight even portions. Arrange a portion of rice into a neat 8cm square, 1cm thick, in the middle of the nori sheet, flattening the rice using an offset palette knife. Spread with 1 tsp of wasabi.

Arrange the prepared veggies in neat layers on top of the rice starting with the spinach, positioning the tofu somewhere in the middle and ending with a layer of pickled ginger. Using damp hands shape another portion of rice into a neat 1cm square the same size as the first and place on top of the ginger. Tightly wrap the nori around the sandwich stack to completely encase – very much like wrapping a parcel. Tightly wrap the clingfilm around the onigirazu. Repeat to make four sushi sandwiches.

Chill for 1 hour before unwrapping. Cut in half using a serrated knife, garnish with mustard cress and serve with extra soy sauce.

ROASTED STUFFED HEIRLOOM TOMATOES

SERVES 4–6

100g long-grain, basmati or
   jasmine rice
2 tbsp olive oil, plus extra
   for drizzling
1 onion, finely chopped
6 large beefsteak or
   heirloom tomatoes
1 fat garlic clove, crushed
1 tsp dried oregano
½ tsp ground cumin
A pinch of crushed dried
   chilli flakes
200–225ml vegetable stock
   or water
50g roasted artichoke hearts
   in oil, drained and roughly
   chopped
50g pitted olives, roughly
   chopped
40g sun- or semi-dried
   tomatoes in oil, drained
   and roughly chopped
50g toasted pine kernels
2 tbsp roughly chopped flat-
   leaf parsley
1 large sprig of bay leaves
2 sprigs of rosemary
2 small red onions, each cut
   into 8 wedges
Salt and freshly ground
   black pepper

Stuffed tomatoes are a somewhat retro dish, but it's time to revisit this Mediterranean classic because they are quite delicious and perfect as part of a summer buffet. Look out for heirloom tomatoes in the height of summer — not only will they look pretty but they are sweet, juicy and full of flavour. Old-school deliciousness and summer on a plate.

Rinse the rice in a sieve under cold running water then soak in fresh water while you prepare the remaining ingredients.

Heat the olive oil in a sauté pan over a low–medium heat, add the finely chopped onion and cook, stirring frequently, for about 10 minutes until softened but not coloured.

Meanwhile, use a serrated knife to cut the top off each tomato. Set the tops aside and use a spoon to scoop the middle and seeds of each tomato into a sieve set over a bowl to catch all the juice. Be careful not to cut through the sides of the tomatoes.

Add the garlic, oregano, cumin and dried chilli flakes to the onions and cook for a further minute. Pour the strained tomato juice into the pan and reduce until almost all of it has evaporated. Roughly chop the tomato middles, discarding the tough cores. Add the tomatoes to the pan and cook for 4–5 minutes until really soft, reduced, thick and jammy.

Drain the rice and add to the pan with 200ml of the stock, season, bring to the boil, reduce the heat to a very gentle simmer, half-cover the pan and cook for 10–12 minutes until the rice is al dente and has absorbed almost all the liquid. Add a little more stock or water if the mixture starts to dry out too much before the rice is cooked.

continues overleaf

Meanwhile, preheat the oven to 160°C fan/180°C/gas mark 4.

Remove the rice mixture from the heat. Add the artichokes, olives and sun-dried tomatoes to the rice mixture with the toasted pine nuts and parsley. Season well and mix to combine. Fill the tomatoes with the rice mixture – if you have a little left over it can be saved for another meal. Pop the tops back on the tomatoes.

Lay the bay and rosemary sprigs in the baking dish and sit the tomatoes on top. Tuck the red onion wedges in around the tomatoes. Drizzle with extra virgin olive oil, pour 4–5 tbsp water around the tomatoes and season. Cover loosely with foil and bake for 30 minutes.

Remove the foil and cook for a further 10–15 minutes until the tomatoes are tender and the edges starting to brown. Serve hot, warm or at room temperature.

LENTILS, LEEKS AND GREENS WITH HERBY COUSCOUS

Sometimes you just want a delicious bowl of veggies, without punchy spices but comforting and full of flavour at the same time. And this is it... served with steaming herby couscous and a drizzle of peppery, fruity oil. In place of baby leaf greens you could use kale, cavolo nero or Savoy cabbage.

SERVES 4

100g dried green lentils,
   rinsed and drained
1 onion, sliced
1 tbsp olive oil
1 fat garlic clove, crushed
2 leeks, trimmed and cut
   into 1cm-thick slices
1 celery stick, trimmed and
   cut into 1cm-thick slices
5 spring onions, trimmed
   and cut into 3cm lengths
500ml vegetable stock
1 bay leaf
100g baby leaf greens,
   trimmed
Salt and freshly ground
   black pepper

FOR THE COUSCOUS
150g couscous
Finely grated zest of
   ½ unwaxed lemon
1 small bunch flat-leaf
   parsley, chopped
50g toasted pine kernels
1 tbsp fruity olive oil or
   avocado oil, to serve

Cook the lentils in a small pan of boiling water for 10–12 minutes until just tender but still with some bite. Remove from the heat and set aside.

Meanwhile, tip the onion into a heavy-based, lidded saucepan or casserole, add the olive oil and cook over a low–medium heat, stirring frequently, for about 8 minutes until tender but not coloured. Add the garlic to the pan and cook for 1 minute. Add the leeks and celery and cook, stirring now and again, for 3–4 minutes until starting to soften. Add the spring onions and cook for a further minute. Add the vegetable stock, bay leaf and salt and freshly ground black pepper. Bring slowly to the boil and simmer for 3–4 minutes.

Drain the lentils and add to the pan. Cover and cook for 15 minutes until the veggies and lentils have softened, adding the baby greens for the last 5 minutes of cooking time.

Meanwhile, soak the couscous in freshly boiled water following the packet instructions – about 10 minutes. Fluff up the grains with a fork, add the lemon zest, chopped parsley and toasted pine kernels and season well with salt and freshly ground black pepper.

Spoon the couscous into bowls, serve the veggies alongside and drizzle with olive or avocado oil to serve.

POTATO AND LENTIL CAKES WITH COLESLAW

MAKES 8/SERVES 4

POTATO AND LENTIL CAKES

500g floury potatoes (about 4 medium)
100g green lentils, rinsed
1 onion, sliced
1 leek, trimmed and sliced
1 tbsp olive oil
1 garlic clove, crushed
1 tsp caraway seeds
1 tsp paprika
1 small bunch flat-leaf parsley, chopped
3 tbsp plain flour
4 tbsp plant-based milk
100g panko breadcrumbs
4 tbsp sunflower oil
Salt and freshly ground black pepper

COLESLAW

1 large carrot, coarsely grated
¼ white or red cabbage, finely shredded
3 spring onions, sliced
1 green chilli, finely chopped
3 tbsp roughly chopped flat-leaf parsley
2 tbsp roughly chopped coriander
2 tbsp pumpkin seeds, toasted
2 tsp poppy seeds
50g pecan nuts, toasted and roughly chopped
2 tbsp vegan mayonnaise, crème fraîche or yogurt
Juice of ½ lemon

Both the potato cakes and coleslaw can be prepared in advance, chilled and then the cakes coated and fried just before serving. Serve with a generous drizzle of chilli sauce and crisp salad leaves or baby leaf spinach.

Cook the whole, unpeeled potatoes in boiling salted water until just tender when tested with a knife. Drain and leave to cool slightly.

In another pan, cook the lentils in boiling water for about 20 minutes until tender, drain and leave to cool.

Meanwhile, tip the onion and leek into a frying pan with the olive oil and cook over a medium heat, stirring frequently, for about 10 minutes until tender and just starting to brown at the edges. Add the garlic, caraway seeds and paprika and cook for another minute. Tip into a large bowl with the cooked lentils and chopped parsley. Coarsely grate the potatoes into the bowl, season well and, using clean hands, mix together until thoroughly combined. Shape the mixture into 8 patties, cover and chill for 20 minutes to firm up. They can be prepared in advance up to this point.

To make the coleslaw, combine the carrot, cabbage, spring onions and chilli in a mixing bowl and add the chopped herbs, seeds and nuts. Half an hour before serving, add the mayonnaise and lemon juice, season well and mix to combine.

When you are ready to cook, tip the flour onto a plate, pour the milk into a shallow bowl and spread the breadcrumbs onto a tray. One at a time, dip the potato cakes first in flour to coat, then in milk and finally in the breadcrumbs.

Heat the sunflower oil in a frying pan over a medium heat and fry the potato cakes, in batches, until crisp and golden brown on both sides and hot all the way through. Remove from the pan and keep warm while you cook the remaining potato cakes.

Serve the potato cakes with the coleslaw and a drizzle of red or green sriracha sauce, if liked.

SPELT WITH SPICED ROASTED CAULIFLOWER

Spelt is a wonderful wholegrain that can be used in much the same way as rice. It absorbs flavours as it cooks, which makes it perfect for risotto-style dishes or salads. The grains have a slightly nutty flavour and almost chewy texture and are a good source of fibre.

SERVES 4–6

1 cauliflower
2 tbsp rapeseed or olive oil
1 tbsp za'atar
1 onion
1 small leek
1 fat garlic clove, crushed
150g pearled spelt
500ml vegetable stock
1 bay leaf
50g blanched hazelnuts, roughly chopped
25g pistachios, roughly chopped
25g pumpkin seeds
50g sultanas
1 tbsp pomegranate molasses
Squeeze of lemon juice
2 tbsp roughly chopped coriander
2 tbsp roughly chopped flat-leaf parsley
2 tbsp pomegranate seeds
Salt and freshly ground black pepper

Preheat the oven to 180° fan/200°C/gas mark 6.

Cut the cauliflower florets and leaves into bite-size pieces. Tip the florets into a large bowl (save the leaves for later), drizzle with 1 tbsp rapeseed oil, add the za'atar and season with salt and freshly ground black pepper. Mix to thoroughly coat the cauliflower in the spices, arrange on a large parchment-lined baking tray and roast in the oven for about 30 minutes, turning after 15 minutes, until tender and starting to brown at the edges.

Meanwhile, cook the spelt. Finely chop the onion and leek, tip into a large saucepan, add 1 tbsp rapeseed oil and cook over a medium heat for about 10 minutes, stirring frequently until softened. Add the garlic and cook for a further minute. Rinse the spelt in a sieve under cold running water and add to the pan with the stock and bay leaf. Season, bring to the boil then reduce the heat and simmer for about 20 minutes or until the spelt is tender and most of the stock has been absorbed.

Add the roughly chopped cauliflower leaves, nuts, pumpkin seeds, sultanas and pomegranate molasses to the cauliflower florets, mix to coat and roast for a further 5 minutes until the leaves are softened and starting to brown at the edges.

Tip the cauliflower mixture into the spelt, add a squeeze of lemon juice and most of the herbs and gently mix to combine. Spoon onto a large platter, scatter with the pomegranate seeds and remaining herbs and serve.

TOMATOES AND RED LENTILS WITH FRESH SPICES
AND GREEN RICE

This is a mood-boosting dish if ever there was one! The contrasting colours of the tomatoes and green rice are enough to make you smile. If cooking this in late summer look out for baby plum tomatoes in a variety of colours — red, gold and yellow. Fresh curry leaves and fenugreek are available in larger supermarkets, Indian grocers or online.

SERVES 4–6

4 banana shallots,
   thinly sliced
2 tbsp olive oil
2 fat garlic cloves, sliced
3 tsp grated fresh ginger
1 fresh red chilli, chopped
2 tsp black mustard seeds
1 tsp cumin seeds
½ tsp ground turmeric
3 tbsp roughly chopped
   fresh fenugreek
   leaves (methi)
20 fresh curry leaves
50g coconut cream
1 small cinnamon stick
3 cardamom pods
100g dried red lentils,
   rinsed and drained
500ml vegetable stock
400g tomatoes, halved
350g baby plum tomatoes
Juice of ½ lime
1 small bunch of coriander,
   roughly chopped
Salt and freshly ground
   black pepper

Tip the shallots into a large sauté pan. Add the olive oil and cook over a low–medium heat for about 5 minutes, stirring almost constantly, until softened and only just starting to turn golden at the edges.

Add the garlic, ginger and chilli and cook for another minute before adding the mustard and cumin seeds, turmeric, fenugreek and curry leaves. Cook for a further minute and then add the coconut cream, cinnamon stick, cardamom, lentils and stock. Add both types of tomatoes to the pan. Bring slowly to the boil, reduce the heat, half-cover the pan with a lid and simmer for about 30 minutes until the lentils are very soft and have thickened the sauce slightly and the tomatoes have cooked down.

Meanwhile, prepare the green rice. Heat the oil in a large saucepan over a low–medium heat, add the onion and cook, stirring often, for about 8 minutes until softened and just starting to brown at the edges. Tip the spinach, kale and coconut cream into a high-powered blender or food processor and whizz to a purée, adding a tablespoon or two of water if needed to make it as smooth as possible.

GREEN RICE

2 tbsp olive oil

1 onion, thinly sliced

125g spinach, washed

100g kale, trimmed and
  washed

100g coconut cream

1 fat garlic clove, crushed

1 fresh green chilli, finely
  chopped

1 tsp cumin seeds

175g basmati rice

350ml vegetable stock

Add the garlic, green chilli and cumin seeds to the onion and cook for a further minute. Tip in the rice and stir to coat in the onion mixture. Pour the spinach purée into the pan along with the vegetable stock, stir well and season well with salt and freshly ground black pepper. Bring to the boil, reduce the heat to a very gentle simmer, cover with a lid and cook for about 12 minutes until the rice is tender and has absorbed almost all the stock.

Add the lime juice and chopped coriander to the tomatoes, season to taste with salt and freshly ground black pepper and serve with the green rice.

ORZO PASTA WITH CHICKPEAS AND GREENS

This one-pan dish can be on the table in under 30 minutes. You can adapt the greens according to the season and your preference: try the leafy cime di rapa (turnip tops/broccoli raab) in autumn, spring greens or shredded sprouts in winter and kale or young leaf spinach in spring or summer. Roughly chopped mint, dill, basil or parsley can also be added to this Mediterranean dish, or try scattering with crumbled vegan feta or Parmesan to serve.

SERVES 4

1 onion, chopped
1 small leek, chopped
1 small celery stick, chopped
2 tbsp fruity olive oil, plus
 extra for drizzling
1 garlic clove, crushed
½ tsp fennel seeds
A pinch of crushed dried
 chilli flakes
1 courgette
125g orzo pasta
1 x 400g can of chickpeas,
 drained and rinsed
600ml vegetable stock
A good handful of peppery
 greens, such as cime
 di rapa, spring greens,
 mustard greens or kale,
 washed and roughly
 shredded
2 tbsp toasted pine kernels
Salt and freshly ground
 black pepper

Tip the onion, leek and celery into a large saucepan with 1 tbsp of the olive oil and cook over a low–medium heat, stirring frequently, until softened. Add the garlic, fennel seeds and chilli flakes and cook for another minute. Meanwhile, coarsely grate the courgette, add to the pan and cook for a further minute until just starting to wilt.

Add the pasta and chickpeas to the pan, mix to combine and add the vegetable stock and season well with salt and freshly ground black pepper. Bring to the boil, reduce the heat to a gentle simmer and cook for 15–20 minutes until the pasta is al dente and has absorbed most of the stock.

Place the greens on top of the chickpeas and pasta, turn off the heat and cover the pan with a lid to allow the greens to steam for 2–3 minutes in the residual heat and the pasta to absorb the remaining liquid.

Add the toasted pine kernels and stir to mix the greens through the pasta and chickpeas.

Drizzle with a little more oil, grind over some extra black pepper and serve.

MUSHROOM, CELERIAC AND PEARL BARLEY STEW

A deliciously earthy dish, perfect for autumnal evenings. Pearl barley thickens the stew and adds a wonderful nuttiness. Select firm mushrooms – a mixture of chestnut and wild is good. Serve with steamed garlicky greens.

SERVES 4–6

1 large onion, chopped
1 carrot, diced
1 leek, trimmed, sliced
 lengthways then cut into
 1cm slices
1 celery stick, trimmed,
 sliced lengthways then
 cut into 1cm slices
2–3 tbsp olive oil
2 garlic cloves, crushed
1 small celeriac, peeled
 and cut into 1.5–2cm dice
 (roughly 350g prepped
 weight)
450g mixed mushrooms
 such as chestnut, shiitake
 or pied de mouton, cut into
 bite-size pieces
750ml vegetable stock
100g pearl barley
2 tsp porcini and white
 truffle paste or white miso
1 bay leaf
1 sprig of thyme
2 tbsp roughly chopped flat-
 leaf parsley, to serve
Salt and freshly ground
 black pepper

Tip the diced onion and carrot into a large, solid casserole. Add the leek and celery with 1 tbsp of the olive oil. Cook the veggies over a low–medium heat for about 8 minutes, stirring frequently, until softened but not coloured.

Add the crushed garlic to the onion mixture and cook for a further minute. Add the diced celeriac and stir to combine, then take off the heat and set aside.

Heat 1 tbsp olive oil in a large frying pan over a high heat, add half the mushrooms and fry until browned. Tip into the casserole and fry the remaining mushrooms, adding more oil if needed, and tip into the casserole. Pour half the vegetable stock into the frying pan to deglaze and stir to lift off any caramelized mushrooms from the bottom of the pan. Pour all the stock into the casserole.

Rinse the pearl barley in a sieve under cold running water, drain and add to the casserole. Add the porcini and truffle paste (or miso), bay leaf and thyme and season well with salt and freshly ground black pepper. Bring slowly to the boil, half cover the pan with a lid and cook for about 40 minutes until all the vegetables and the pearl barley are tender.

Scatter with chopped parsley to serve.

MAPO TOFU

For this classic Sichuan dish you need to use medium rather than extra firm or silken tofu. Medium tofu will hold its shape (just) while remaining silky and soft, and provide a cooling balance to the hot hot hot sauce. Fried mushrooms add an earthy depth to the sauce, while Sichuan peppercorns lend their characteristic tongue-tingling flavour and heat.

SERVES 2

300g medium tofu, cut into
   3cm cubes
2 tsp Sichuan peppercorns
2 tbsp sunflower oil
150g king oyster or shiitake
   mushrooms, chopped into
   1cm pieces
1 fat garlic clove, crushed
½ fresh red chilli, finely
   chopped
3 tsp grated fresh ginger
3 spring onions, white and
   green parts separated
   and sliced
1 tbsp Sichuan chilli bean
   paste
1 tbsp Shaoxing wine
½ tbsp fermented black
   beans, rinsed and roughly
   chopped
2 tsp cornflour
Steamed rice, to serve

Blanch the tofu cubes by covering them in just-boiled water for 10 minutes, then drain.

Toast the peppercorns in a dry wok over a medium heat for 30 seconds until starting to smoke and smell aromatic. Tip into a mortar and coarsely grind using the pestle.

Meanwhile, heat the oil in the wok over medium heat, add the mushrooms and cook, stirring frequently, for about 10 minutes until soft, reduced and deep brown. Add the ground peppercorns, garlic, chilli, ginger and white parts of the spring onions and stir-fry for 30 seconds.

Add the chilli bean paste, Shaoxing wine and black beans and continue to stir-fry for 30 seconds. Pour in 200ml water, bring the boil and simmer for 1 minute. Add the drained tofu and stir gently to coat.

In a small bowl mix the cornflour with 1 tbsp water, pour into the wok, stir to combine and then simmer until the sauce thickens. Scatter with the chopped green parts of the spring onions and serve immediately with steamed rice.

ROASTED SPROUTS AND CABBAGE
WITH GOCHUJANG, GINGER AND SESAME

When I first created this recipe I ate almost the whole tray of veggies, as soon as they were cooked, straight from the tin... no waiting to cool down and no sharing. Ordinarily I would eat this seated at the table, stirred through noodles or with steamed rice.

SERVES 2

200g Brussels sprouts,
  trimmed and halved
1 pointed (hispi) cabbage,
  trimmed, halved and cut
  into wedges 2–3cm thick
2 tbsp sunflower oil
½ tsp ground turmeric
1 tbsp agave syrup
2–3 tsp freshly grated ginger
1 fat garlic clove, crushed
1 heaped tbsp gochujang
  paste
1 tbsp soy sauce
2–3 tsp sesame seeds
2 tbsp roughly chopped
  coriander
Salt and freshly ground
  black pepper

Preheat the oven to 180°C fan/200°C/gas mark 6 and line a large shallow roasting tin with foil.

Tip the sprouts and cabbage into the lined tin, drizzle with 1 tbsp oil and season with salt and freshly ground black pepper.

Roast on the middle shelf of the oven for about 20 minutes until the veg are starting to soften and brown; the timing will depend on the size of your sprouts and thickness of the cabbage wedges. If they are looking a little pale after 20 minutes cook for a further 5 minutes.

Meanwhile, in a small bowl combine the remaining oil, turmeric, agave, ginger, garlic, gochujang and soy sauce. Loosen with 1–2 tbsp water to give a coating consistency.

Spoon the mixture over the sprouts and cabbage, scatter with sesame seeds and return to the oven for a further 5 minutes until the veggies are tender and a deep, golden brown.

Scatter with coriander and serve with rice or noodles.

SOFT ROASTED AUBERGINES
WITH SOY DRESSING

For this dish you can cook the aubergines one of two ways. Either bake in a hot oven until very soft or cook over a griddle pan — just remember to turn on the extractor fan and open a window. Leave the aubergines to cool in the dressing before serving with some steamed rice.

SERVES 2

2 aubergines
2 tsp freshly grated ginger
2 tbsp soy sauce
1 tbsp mirin
1 tbsp rice vinegar or
   lime juice
2 spring onions, shredded
1 tsp toasted sesame seeds

Preheat the oven to 200°C fan/220°C/gas mark 7 or preheat a griddle pan over a medium–high heat.

If cooking the aubergines in the oven arrange them in a small roasting tin and cook on the middle shelf, for about 30 minutes, turning halfway through, until the skin is almost blackened and the flesh tender, juicy and soft. If cooking on a griddle simply place the whole aubergines on the hot griddle and cook for about 5 minutes on each side and for about 15 minutes in total, turning frequently, until the skin is blackened and crisp in places and the flesh is very soft and starting to slump.

Leave the aubergines to cool then remove the stalk and skin. Slice into rounds about 3–4cm thick and arrange in a serving dish.

Combine the ginger, soy sauce, mirin and vinegar in a small bowl. Pour over the aubergines, cover and chill for 1 hour. Chill the shredded spring onions at the same time.

Scatter the aubergines with sesame seeds and serve topped with the spring onions.

CURRIED CAULIFLOWER LAKSA

A delicious bowl of warming golden laksa is perfect supper any time of the year. The paste can be made in a matter of moments but if speed is of the essence you could always use a jar of ready-made, good-quality laksa paste — just check that it doesn't contain fish sauce or shrimp paste. This recipe makes more paste than you need for four bowls of laksa but any leftovers will keep well in a sealed container in the fridge for 2 weeks or in the freezer for 2 months. The roasted cauliflower is seasoned with curry powder and garlic granules — the latter are a wonderful way of getting a hit of garlic flavour without it burning during the blast of oven heat. They are also a great seasoning for roast potatoes… just saying. Tofu puffs are available in Asian supermarkets but easy to make yourself. They add texture and protein to this soup.

SERVES 4

LAKSA PASTE
2–3 dried whole chillies
   or 1 large fresh red fresh
   chilli, roughly chopped
2 stalks lemongrass,
   trimmed and roughly
   chopped
4cm piece fresh ginger,
   peeled and roughly
   chopped
2 fat garlic cloves, chopped
4 small shallots, chopped
2 tsp ground coriander
1 tsp ground turmeric
1 tsp tomato purée
25g unsalted cashews
100g block creamed coconut

½ cauliflower, cut into bite-
   size pieces
1–2 tbsp sunflower oil
1 tsp medium curry powder

continues overleaf

Start by making the laksa paste. If using dried chillies, soak them in a small bowl of freshly boiled water for about 10 minutes until soft. Put the fresh chilli (if using), lemongrass, ginger, garlic and shallots in a small food processor. Drain the chillies, roughly chop and add to the processor with the spices, tomato purée and cashews. Add 1 tbsp of the creamed coconut and blend to a smooth paste.

Preheat the oven to 160°C fan/180°C/gas mark 4.

Tip the cauliflower into a bowl. Add the oil, curry powder, chilli flakes, garlic granules and salt and freshly ground black pepper. Mix well to coat the cauliflower in the spices. Scatter the florets on a baking tray and roast in the oven for about 20 minutes until tender and starting to brown at the edges.

Meanwhile, make the tofu puffs, if not using store-bought. Cut the tofu into 2cm dice and pat dry on kitchen paper. Heat 6 tbsp of oil in a deep saucepan over a medium heat until a small piece of tofu sizzles on contact with the hot oil. Carefully add the diced tofu to the hot oil and fry for about 2 minutes, stirring frequently until crisp, puffy and golden. Remove from the pan with a slotted spoon and drain on kitchen paper. Pour off all but 2 tbsp of the oil from the pan.

continues overleaf

1 tsp crushed dried
   chilli flakes
1 tsp garlic granules
Salt and freshly ground
   black pepper
1 litre vegetable stock
2–3 tsp soft light brown
   sugar or coconut sugar
Juice of ½ lime
Soy sauce

TO SERVE
100g firm tofu or 8 store-
   bought tofu puffs
2–6 tbsp sunflower oil
200g flat rice noodles
100g beansprouts
4 sprigs of fresh coriander
1 large fresh red
   chilli, sliced
2 spring onions, sliced
4 lime wedges

Cook the noodles in boiling water following the packet instructions. Place the saucepan in which you cooked the tofu over a medium heat (or, if you haven't made your own tofu puffs, then add 2 tbsp oil to a saucepan). Add 3 tbsp laksa paste and stirring constantly cook for about 4 minutes until very fragrant. Add the vegetable stock and crumble in the remaining creamed coconut, stir well and slowly bring to the boil. Simmer for 3–4 minutes then taste and add sugar, lime juice, salt and soy sauce as needed to balance the flavours.

Drain the noodles and divide between 4 deep bowls, pour over the broth and top with the roasted cauliflower, tofu puffs and a small handful of beansprouts. Garnish with a sprig of coriander, sliced chillies, spring onions and a wedge of lime.

ORECCHIETTE WITH BUTTERNUT SQUASH, BRUSSELS SPROUTS
AND PECAN CRUNCH

This is a wonderful autumnal dish. The pecan crunch and roasted squash can both be prepared ahead, making assembling this dish a doddle. You could use any orange-fleshed pumpkin here, but do remove the skin from the tougher varieties (butternut squash doesn't need peeling). Brussels sprouts have a sweet, nutty flavour that works so well with butternut squash and pecans, but feel free to use shredded spring greens or kale if you prefer, and swap the pecans for walnuts.

SERVES 4

600g butternut squash
   (about 1 small)
5 tbsp olive oil
½ tsp crushed dried
   chilli flakes
½ tsp garlic granules
50g pecan nuts
25g pumpkin seeds
2 tsp nutritional yeast
2 tsp dried breadcrumbs
8–10 sage leaves, shredded
250g orecchiette or other
   small pasta
300g Brussels sprouts,
   trimmed and shredded
1 garlic clove, crushed
2 tbsp chopped flat-leaf
   parsley
Salt and freshly ground
   black pepper

Preheat the oven to 170°C fan/190°C/gas mark 5 and line a large baking tray or shallow roasting tin with foil.

Wash the butternut squash, cut in half lengthways, remove the seeds and fibres and slice into 3mm-thick half-moons. Tip into a large bowl, add 2 tbsp of the olive oil, the chilli flakes and garlic granules and season well with salt and freshly ground black pepper. Using your hands, mix well to coat the squash slices in seasoning and oil. Spread out in the lined tin and roast for about 30 minutes until softened and starting to brown at the edges.

Meanwhile, bring a large pan of salted water to the boil. Tip the pecans and pumpkin seeds onto a small baking tray and toast in the oven for about 4 minutes until crisp. Roughly chop the nuts and seeds, tip into a bowl, add 2 tsp olive oil, the nutritional yeast, breadcrumbs and seasoning. Mix, return to the baking tray and bake for another minute until crisp.

Add the shredded sage to the butternut squash, mix gently to combine and return to the oven for a further 5 minutes.

Cook the pasta in the boiling water according to the packet instructions. Meanwhile, heat 1 tbsp olive oil in a large frying pan over a medium–high heat, add the sprouts and cook, stirring almost constantly for about 4 minutes until wilted, tender and just starting to turn golden at the edges. Add the crushed garlic, season well and cook for a further minute.

Use a slotted spoon to scoop the pasta from the water directly into the frying pan, add the squash and chopped parsley and mix, adding a little pasta water if needed to combine. Serve scattered with the nut and seed crunch.

SMOKY AUBERGINE WITH TOMATO AND CHICKPEAS

By roasting aubergines you use far less oil than if you were to fry them. The smokiness in the sauce comes from chipotle chillies, which in this instance are dried and rehydrated. You can use chipotle paste if you prefer — add it cautiously though, a teaspoon at a time, as it can vary in heat. Serve with steamed couscous, brown basmati rice or warmed Quick Flatbreads (see page 158).

SERVES 4

2 dried chipotle chillies
1 large onion, chopped
3 tbsp olive oil
500g ripe tomatoes
2 aubergines, quartered
  lengthways then cut into
  large bite-size chunks
2 Romano peppers,
  deseeded and cut into large
  bite-size chunks
1 large garlic clove, crushed
1 tsp ground cumin
2 tbsp tomato purée
1 x 400g can of chickpeas,
  drained and rinsed
200ml vegetable stock
2 tsp date or dark agave
  syrup
Salt and freshly ground
  black pepper

TO SERVE

2 tbsp roughly chopped
  coriander
Zest of 1 unwaxed lemon

Preheat the oven to 160° fan/180°C/gas mark 4.

Soak the chipotle chillies in freshly boiled water for 20 minutes to soften.

Tip the chopped onion into a large, heavy saucepan with a lid. Add 1 tbsp of the olive oil and cook over a low–medium heat for about 8 minutes until softened and just starting to brown at the edges.

Meanwhile, cut a cross on the underside of each tomato and soak in a bowl of freshly boiled water for 1 minute to loosen the skins. Drain the tomatoes under cold running water, peel off the skins, cut out the tough core and roughly chop the flesh. Set aside.

Combine the aubergine and peppers in a large roasting tin, drizzle with the remaining olive oil and mix thoroughly to coat the vegetables in oil. Cook in the oven for about 30 minutes, turning every 10 minutes, until softened and golden brown.

Add the garlic and cumin to the onions and cook for another minute. Drain the chipotle chillies, finely chop and add to the saucepan with the tomato purée. Stir to combine and cook for a further 2 minutes to lightly caramelize the tomato purée. Add the chopped tomatoes, chickpeas and vegetable stock and season well with salt and freshly ground black pepper. Bring to the boil, reduce the heat and simmer for 10 minutes until the tomatoes have broken down and softened.

Add the roasted aubergines and peppers to the pan, cover and continue to cook for a further 10 minutes until the aubergines are very soft and have soaked up the tomato sauce. Add the date syrup and adjust the seasoning if needed. Scatter with the coriander and lemon zest to serve.

ROASTED CAULI AND CORN TACOS

Tacos are a fun and easy way to feed a crowd; all the fillings can be prepared ahead of time and heated as needed. Add some crunchy iceberg lettuce, grated carrot or vegan cheese if you like, and serve with hot sauce.

SERVES 4

1 small cauliflower, cut into small florets, smaller leaves reserved

100g sweetcorn kernels, fresh or frozen and defrosted

1 tbsp olive oil

1 tsp dried oregano

1 tsp garlic granules

½ tsp ground cumin

½ tsp ancho chilli powder

1 red onion, thinly sliced into half-moons

3 tbsp cider or white wine vinegar

1 tsp salt

1 tsp caster sugar

A pinch of crushed dried chilli flakes

1 tbsp finely chopped sliced jalapeños from a jar, drained, plus extra to serve

4 heaped tbsp vegan mayonnaise or soured cream

8 tbsp refried beans

6–8 small soft flour tortillas

1 large avocado, halved, stoned and sliced

12 cherry tomatoes, quartered

Lime wedges and fresh coriander leaves, to serve

Salt and freshly ground black pepper

Preheat the oven to 170°C fan/190°C/gas mark 5 and line a baking tray with foil or baking paper.

Tip the cauliflower florets onto the baking tray with the sweetcorn kernels, olive oil, oregano, garlic granules, cumin and ancho chilli powder. Season well with salt and freshly ground black pepper and use your hands to mix to combine. Spread out the veggies in a single layer and roast for about 30 minutes, turning halfway through, until tender and starting to turn golden brown at the edges. Add the reserved cauliflower leaves for the last 5 minutes of cooking time.

Meanwhile, pickle the red onion. Tip the slices into a bowl, add the vinegar, salt, sugar, chilli flakes and 1 tbsp freshly boiled water. Mix to combine, set aside for 30–40 minutes to soften and then drain off the excess pickling liquid.

Mix the finely chopped jalapeños with the mayonnaise or soured cream. Heat the refried beans, either in a small pan over a low heat or in the microwave following the packet instructions.

Wrap the tortillas in foil and warm in the oven for 5 minutes. Meanwhile, fill bowls with the toppings so that everyone can construct their tacos. Spread a spoonful of warmed refried beans onto each tortilla and top with sliced avocado, roasted cauli and sweetcorn, cherry tomatoes, pickled red onions and a good spoonful of jalapeño mayo. Scatter with coriander leaves, squeeze over fresh lime juice and serve with napkins!

FEASTS

BUTTERNUT SQUASH NUT ROAST

This glorious dish would be perfect to serve at a festive meal, such as Christmas or Thanksgiving. The butternut squash is roasted and then filled with rice, nuts and dried fruit and baked again on a bed of woody herbs. The squash can be fully prepared in advance, the halves filled and chilled until ready to bake. If you like, serve with Tomato Kasundi on page 145.

SERVES 4–6

1 butternut squash
2½ tbsp olive oil, plus extra
  for drizzling
1 large onion, finely chopped
1 leek, trimmed and finely
  chopped
125g chestnut mushrooms,
  quartered
2 fat garlic cloves, crushed
100g brown basmati rice,
  rinsed and drained
300ml vegetable stock
75g cooked chestnuts,
  roughly chopped
50g walnut pieces, toasted
50g hazelnuts, toasted and
  roughly chopped
50g dried cranberries
1 tbsp balsamic vinegar
3 tbsp chopped flat-leaf
  parsley
1 bushy sprig of thyme,
  leaves picked
2 bushy sprigs of bay leaves
2 bushy sprigs of rosemary
2 tbsp breadcrumbs
1 tbsp grated vegan Italian-
  style cheese
Salt and freshly ground
  black pepper

Preheat the oven to 170°C fan/190°C/gas mark 5.

Cut the butternut squash in half lengthways and place, cut side up, in a smallish roasting tin. Scrape out the seeds and fibres, score the flesh, season, drizzle with 1 tbsp of the olive oil, cover with foil and roast for about 45 minutes until the flesh is tender all the way through when tested with the point of a knife.

Meanwhile, prepare the filling. Tip the onion and leek into a sauté pan, add 1½ tbsp olive oil and cook over a low–medium heat, stirring often, until softened and just starting to turn golden at the edges.

Add the mushrooms and garlic to the pan, stir to combine and cook for a further 5 minutes until the mushrooms are tender. Tip in the drained rice, pour in the stock and season well with salt and freshly ground black pepper.

Cover the pan with a disc of baking paper, or half-cover with a lid, and simmer very gently for about 30 minutes until the rice is al dente and there is still a little stock remaining in the pan. Remove from the heat and tip into a large bowl.

Add the chestnuts, walnuts, hazelnuts, cranberries, balsamic vinegar, parsley and thyme leaves to the rice mixture. Use a spoon to scoop out the cooked flesh from the butternut squash halves, keeping the skin intact and leaving a shell of about 1cm thick on all sides. Roughly chop the squash, add to the rice and season well.

Lay the bay leaves and rosemary sprigs in the roasting tin and place the butternut squash halves on top. Spoon the rice mixture to fill each half – any left over can be cooked alongside in another baking tin. Cover with foil and bake for 30–35 minutes until piping hot. Remove the foil, scatter with breadcrumbs, Italian-style cheese and drizzle with olive oil and return to the oven for a further 10 minutes until crisp. Cut into slices and serve.

MALLOREDDUS WITH TOMATOES, GREEN BEANS AND BASIL

Fresh homemade pasta is so delicious and easy to make — it simply requires good-quality pasta flour and an hour or so of quiet kitchen time. Malloreddus pasta are little gnocchi shapes, which are easily made by rolling the pasta pieces down the tines of a fork or by using a ridged wooden pasta paddle for a slightly more professional finish. If the mood takes you, add a few finely chopped sun-dried tomatoes, olives or capers to the sauce.

SERVES 4

PASTA
200g fine semolina flour,
   plus extra for rolling
50g '00' grade pasta flour
1 tsp salt
2 tbsp olive oil
130–150ml water

SAUCE
4 tbsp extra virgin olive oil,
   plus extra for drizzling
2 fat garlic cloves, crushed
A pinch of crushed dried
   chilli flakes
A pinch of fennel seeds
1 x 400g can of good-quality
   plum tomatoes
12 cherry tomatoes, halved
150g fine green beans,
   trimmed and halved
A small bunch of basil,
   leaves picked and torn
Salt and freshly ground
   black pepper

TO SERVE
1 tbsp pine kernels, toasted
Pangrattato (see page 155)

Start by making the pasta dough. Tip both flours into a large mixing bowl, add the salt, mix to combine and make a well in the middle. Add the olive oil and 130ml water and mix using a fork, flicking the dry ingredients into the liquid. Add more water, a teaspoon at a time, if needed to bring the dough together into a ball.

Turn the dough onto a very lightly floured wooden board or work surface and knead for about 5 minutes until smooth. Return it to the bowl, cover and leave at room temperature for 30 minutes for the gluten to rest and relax.

Cut off one-sixth of the dough and on a very lightly floured surface roll into a rope about 1cm thick. Cut the rope into 1cm pieces and roll each piece down the tines of a fork (or a wooden gnocchi paddle), pressing gently with your thumb as you roll. Tumble the pasta shapes onto a tray lined with a clean tea towel that you have lightly dusted with semolina flour.

Continue rolling the shapes until all the dough has been used up. Leave the pasta to dry at room temperature for a couple of hours.

When you are ready to eat, place a large pan of water over high heat, add 2 tsp salt and bring to the boil.

continues overleaf

Meanwhile, heat the extra virgin olive oil in a large sauté pan over a medium heat, add the garlic, chilli flakes and fennel seeds and cook, stirring, for about 1 minute. Do not allow the garlic to brown. Add the plum tomatoes to the pan and use a wooden spoon to crush them into pieces. Continue to cook for 7–10 minutes until the tomatoes have broken up and reduced into a sauce. Add the cherry tomatoes and cook for a further 2 minutes to soften. Season well.

Drop the beans into the boiling water and cook for 2 minutes until tender. Using a slotted spoon, scoop them out of the water and into the tomato sauce.

Tip the malloreddus into the boiling water and cook for 2–3 minutes until tender and the pieces float to the surface. Using the slotted spoon scoop the pasta from the water and into the tomato pan. Mix gently, add the torn basil leaves and spoon onto warmed plates.

Serve with a drizzle of extra virgin olive oil, toasted pine kernels and pangrattato to sprinkle over.

JACKFRUIT BAO BUNS

Who doesn't love soft, slightly chewy, pillowy bao buns? Filled with sticky, soy-glazed jackfruit and crisp vegetables, these are real crowd-pleasers. Canned jackfruit is now readily available in most large supermarkets and, like tofu, it is particularly delicious stir-fried. If you prefer, swap it for cauliflower florets or tofu – or try filling the bao buns with the Teriyaki Aubergine and King Oyster Mushrooms on page 15. A large, double-layered bamboo steamer is ideal for cooking the bao buns. You can get four buns on each layer of the steamer, so they can all be cooked at the same time.

MAKES 8

BAO BUNS

250g plain flour

2 tsp caster sugar

1 tsp easy-blend
   dried yeast

½ tsp salt

½ tsp baking powder

50ml plant milk

75ml water

1 tbsp rice vinegar

2 tsp sesame oil, plus extra
   for brushing

2 tsp black sesame seeds

FILLING

2 x 400g cans of jackfruit

1 tbsp sunflower oil

2 garlic cloves, finely
   chopped

4cm piece fresh ginger,
   finely chopped

1 red chilli, deseeded
   and finely chopped

6 spring onions,
   4 thinly sliced

3 tbsp soy sauce

2 tbsp hoisin sauce

2 tbsp maple syrup

1½ tbsp rice vinegar

1 tsp Chinese five-spice

1 carrot

¼ cucumber

½ red pepper

Leaves from a small bunch
   of coriander, to serve

Combine the flour, sugar, yeast, salt and baking powder in the bowl of a stand mixer fitted with a dough hook. Heat the milk and water to lukewarm, add the rice vinegar and sesame oil and tip into the dry ingredients. Mix on low speed until incorporated and then continue kneading for about 4 minutes until the dough is silky smooth. Shape the dough into a ball, return to the bowl, cover and leave at room temperature for about 1 hour or until doubled in size.

Cut two circles of baking parchment the same diameter as the inside of the steamer baskets. Fold each paper disc in half, and then in half again to make a triangle, then fold this triangle in half again. Snip small sections out of each folded edge so that when you open the paper it is dotted with small holes. Lay a disc in the bottom of each steamer basket.

Weigh the bao dough and divide it into 8 even portions. Shape each portion into a neat ball with the seam on the underside. Working one at a time, roll each dough ball into an oval shape – roughly the size of your hand – and 5mm thick. Brush with sesame oil and fold in half. Brush the top with sesame oil and sprinkle with black sesame seeds. Place the buns in the steamer to prove, leaving space between each bun and the edge of the steamer. Stack the steamer baskets together, cover with the lid and leave for about 1 hour at room temperature until the buns have nearly doubled in size.

Meanwhile, prepare the filling. Drain the jackfruit and squeeze out any excess water. Heat the sunflower oil in a large frying pan or wok, add the jackfruit and fry over a medium heat for about 10 minutes until golden brown, breaking up the pieces slightly with a wooden spoon.

continues overleaf

Add the garlic, ginger, chilli and 4 sliced spring onions to the pan and continue frying for another minute. In a small bowl combine the soy and hoisin sauces, maple syrup, rice vinegar and Chinese five-spice with 4 tbsp water. Pour into the pan, mix to combine, reduce the heat slightly and continue to cook for a further 3 minutes or so until the jackfruit is caramelized and coated in sticky sauce. Remove from the heat while you prepare the remaining filling ingredients.

Using a julienne grater, cut the carrot and cucumber into fine strips. Finely slice the red pepper and remaining 2 spring onions. Cover and chill until ready to assemble the bao buns.

Fill a large frying pan or wok with water to a depth of about 5cm and bring to the boil over a medium heat. Place the stacked steamer over the water and cook the bao buns for 10–12 minutes until the surface of the buns is firm, the middles puffy and they have doubled in size.

Divide the jackfruit filling and shredded vegetables between the buns, scatter with coriander leaves and serve.

TERIYAKI TOFU BALLS

Use smoked or plain tofu to make these flavour-packed balls, which can be fried in advance, making them perfect to serve at a gathering. Simply reheat on a baking tray in a moderate oven. Serve with stir-fried green vegetables and steamed rice.

MAKES 24/SERVES 4—6

225g extra firm tofu
1 tbsp ground flax seed
6 spring onions, trimmed
    and thinly sliced
1 fat garlic clove, crushed
3 tsp grated fresh ginger
1 red chilli, chopped
1 tbsp sunflower oil, plus
    extra for deep-frying
150g shiitake mushrooms or
    a mix of shiitake and oyster
    mushrooms, chopped into
    1cm pieces
75g cashews, chopped
50g kale, shredded
1 sheet of nori, toasted
2 tbsp soy sauce
1 tbsp white miso or tahini
2 tbsp toasted sesame seeds
50g panko breadcrumbs
Coriander leaves, to serve

SAUCE

4cm piece fresh ginger,
    finely shredded
3 spring onions, trimmed
    and thinly sliced
100ml soy sauce
3 tbsp mirin
2 tbsp maple syrup
1 tbsp rice vinegar
2 tsp cornflour
1—2 tsp chilli oil

Drain the tofu and pat dry on kitchen paper. Cut the tofu into small dice and set aside. In a small bowl mix the ground flax seed with 3 tbsp cold water and set that aside too.

Have all your vegetables prepared before you start. Tip the spring onions into a wok and add the garlic, ginger and chilli. Add the sunflower oil and cook over a medium heat for 30 seconds until starting to soften. Add the mushrooms and cook, stirring constantly, for a minute until they too start to soften. Add the cashews and kale, stir well to combine, cook for a further 30 seconds and remove from the heat. Add the tofu, crumble in the toasted nori sheet, then add the soy sauce, miso, sesame seeds and breadcrumbs.

Tip everything into a food processor and pulse until finely chopped and the mixture starts to clump together. Add the soaked flax seed and pulse again to combine. Using your hands roll the mixture into 24 firm, neat balls the size of walnuts, cover and chill for 30 minutes.

Heat sunflower oil to a depth of 4cm in a wok or sauté pan over a medium–high heat. Cook the tofu balls in batches of 3 or 4 for about 2 minutes until golden brown. (Do not add too many to the pan at once, otherwise they will simmer rather than fry in the oil.) Drain on kitchen paper and keep warm in a low oven while you cook the remaining balls.

Meanwhile, prepare the sauce. Tip the ginger and spring onions into a small saucepan. Pour in the soy sauce, mirin, maple syrup, rice vinegar and 150ml water. Bring to the boil and simmer for 20 seconds. In a small bowl mix the cornflour with 1 tbsp of water until smooth. Add to the sauce, whisk to combine and simmer for 30 seconds until thickened and glossy. Add chilli oil to taste.

Serve the hot tofu balls with the sauce spooned over to coat, sprinkled with coriander leaves.

ROAST SQUASH, 'PANEER' AND FAVA BEANS
IN MAKHANI SAUCE

The base for this delicious curry resembles that used for classic Indian butter chicken – without the butter or the chicken! You will make more of it than you need for this recipe but as the ingredients list is long it's worth making this bigger quantity. The sauce freezes brilliantly, and no one ever complains about having delicious curry sauce in the freezer... Fried tofu is remarkably similar to the Indian cheese paneer; both are slightly 'squeaky', so the tofu is a brilliant vegan sub here. Dried fava beans need soaking overnight so do plan ahead. They have a wonderful rich, deep flavour but if hard to find they can be swapped for green or brown lentils or dried borlotti beans.

SERVES 6

100g dried fava beans,
  soaked overnight in a large
  bowl of cold water
1 tsp cumin seeds
1 tsp fenugreek seeds
Seeds from 6 cardamom
  pods
1 tsp chilli powder
1 tsp garam masala
½ tsp ground turmeric
2 tbsp coconut oil
2 onions, sliced
3 garlic cloves, crushed
4cm piece fresh ginger,
  grated
1 green chilli, finely
  chopped
1 red chilli, finely chopped
2 heaped tbsp tomato purée
500g fresh tomatoes,
  chopped

Drain the soaked fava beans and rinse under cold running water. Set aside.

Toast the cumin, fenugreek and cardamom seeds in a small dry frying pan over a medium heat for 30 seconds until aromatic and toasty. Grind the seeds using a pestle and mortar. Add the chilli powder, garam masala and turmeric and set aside.

Melt the coconut oil in heavy saucepan over a low–medium heat, add the onions and cook, stirring frequently, until softened and starting to lightly brown at the edges. Add the garlic, ginger and red and green chillies and cook for a minute. Add the spices and cook for a further minute, stirring frequently. Add the tomato purée, stirring frequently, and cook for 2 minutes until just starting to caramelize on the bottom of the pan. Add the fresh and tinned tomatoes, bay leaves, cinnamon stick and sugar and season well with salt and freshly ground black pepper. Bring to the boil, reduce to a gentle simmer, half-cover the pan with a lid and cook for 40–45 minutes, stirring frequently, until thickened. Add the cashews for the last 5 minutes of cooking time.

Meanwhile, preheat the oven to 180°C fan/200°C/gas mark 6.

Tip the drained fava beans into a small saucepan and cover with water. Bring to a simmer and cook for 35–40 minutes until just tender. Leave to cool.

1 x 400g can of chopped
   tomatoes
2 bay leaves
1 cinnamon stick
1 tsp soft brown sugar
50g unsalted cashews,
   chopped, plus extra
   for garnish
650g butternut squash,
   peeled and deseeded
   weight, cut into bite-size
   pieces
2 tbsp sunflower oil
175g extra firm tofu, drained
   and patted dry on kitchen
   paper
200ml coconut cream
Small bunch of fresh
   coriander
Salt and freshly ground
   black pepper

Tip the butternut squash onto a baking tray, coat in 1 tbsp of the sunflower oil, season and roast for about 25 minutes, turning halfway through, until starting to soften.

Cut the tofu into 2cm dice. Heat the remaining sunflower oil in a frying pan over a high heat, add the tofu and fry until golden brown all over. Remove from the pan and set aside.

Remove the bay leaves and cinnamon stick from the curry sauce and blend the sauce until smooth using a stick blender. Taste and add seasoning or a little sugar as needed. Spoon off half the curry sauce and set aside to cool for use another time. Add most of the coconut cream and 100–150ml water to the remaining sauce in the pan and return to a low heat, stirring to combine. Add the roasted squash, fried tofu and drained cooked fava beans and mix gently. Half-cover the pan with a lid and cook over a low heat for 5 minutes to allow all the curry flavours to mingle with the ingredients.

Drizzle over a little more coconut cream and scatter with roughly chopped toasted cashews and fresh coriander leaves to serve.

RICE AND LENTILS WITH TAHINI ROASTED ROOT VEG
AND CHERMOULA DRESSING

Don't be put off by the long list of ingredients here: many of them are store-cupboard items. This recipe is inspired by, and borrows elements from, two staple dishes in which rice is cooked with lentils and caramelized onions — Egyptian koshari and Middle Eastern mujaddara. Pomegranate seeds are often used to lend a note of tart sweetness to savoury rice but you could replace them with a tablespoon of sour barberries or dried cranberries if you prefer.

SERVES 6

2 onions, thinly sliced

4–5 tbsp olive oil

A good pinch of saffron stamens

100g Puy lentils

5 medium parsnips, peeled and quartered lengthways

5 carrots, peeled and quartered lengthways

5 medium beetroots, trimmed and quartered (no need to peel)

2 tsp cumin seeds

2 tsp coriander seeds

1 tsp Aleppo chilli flakes

½ tsp garlic granules

2 garlic cloves, crushed

300g brown basmati rice, rinsed

200g cooked chickpeas, drained and rinsed

500ml vegetable stock

1 bay leaf

1 cinnamon stick

continues overleaf

Start by cooking the rice. Tip the onions into a heavy, lidded saucepan, add 2 tbsp olive oil and cook slowly over a low–medium heat for about 30 minutes, stirring frequently, until very soft and starting to caramelize at the edges. Soak the saffron in 2 tbsp freshly boiled water in a small bowl.

Preheat the oven to 180°C fan/200°C/gas mark 6 and line one large or two smaller baking trays with baking paper.

Meanwhile, rinse the lentils and cook in a pan of boiling water for about 20 minutes until just tender but still with a little 'bite'. Drain and set aside.

Combine the prepared root veg in a large bowl. Lightly crush the cumin seeds, coriander seeds and Aleppo chilli flakes using a pestle and mortar. Add to the veggies with the garlic granules and 2–3 tbsp olive oil. Season well with salt and freshly ground black pepper and mix well to thoroughly coat the vegetables in spices.

Arrange in a single layer on the lined baking tray(s) and roast for about 45 minutes, turning halfway through, until tender and browning at the edges.

Meanwhile, add the crushed garlic to the onions and cook for a further minute. Add the rice to the pan, along with the drained lentils and chickpeas. Pour the veg stock and saffron, with its soaking water, into the pan, add the bay leaf and cinnamon stick and season well with salt and freshly ground black pepper. Bring to the boil, cover with a lid and reduce

continues overleaf

2 tbsp tahini

2 tbsp maple syrup

Seeds of ½ pomegranate

Leaves from a small bunch
  of coriander

Salt and freshly ground
  black pepper

CHERMOULA DRESSING

1 tsp cumin seeds

½ tsp coriander seeds

1 fat garlic clove, roughly
  chopped

1 mild green chilli (such as
  fresh jalapeño), sliced

2 spring onions, trimmed
  and sliced

25g flat-leaf parsley, leaves
  and stalks, very roughly
  chopped

25g coriander, leaves
  and stalks, very roughly
  chopped

Juice of ½ lemon

½ tsp ground sumac

½ tsp cayenne pepper

6 tbsp extra virgin olive oil

the heat to its lowest setting. Cook for about 30 minutes until the rice is tender and the stock has been absorbed. Remove from the heat and leave covered until ready to serve.

To prepare the chermoula dressing, toast the cumin and coriander seeds in a dry frying pan over a medium heat for 1 minute until starting to brown and smell aromatic. Tip into a small food processor, along with all the remaining ingredients. Season with salt and freshly ground black pepper and whizz until nearly smooth.

In a small bowl mix together the tahini and maple syrup, spoon over the roasted veggies, mix to coat and return to the oven for a further 5 minutes until golden and sticky.

Spoon the rice onto a large platter, remove the bay leaf and cinnamon stick, and arrange the roasted veggies on top. Scatter with pomegranate seeds and coriander leaves and serve with the chermoula dressing for drizzling.

ROAST TOMATO RISOTTO

Roasting tomatoes really intensifies their flavour, making them perfect for stirring through pasta, gnocchi, rice and other grains. Make this risotto in the height of summer when tomatoes are plentiful and tasting their very best.

SERVES 4

200g cherry or baby plum
tomatoes
4 tomatoes, halved
horizontally
2 tbsp extra virgin olive oil
A pinch of crushed dried
chilli flakes (optional)
1 large sprig of thyme
1 onion, finely chopped
½ fennel bulb, finely
chopped
2 tbsp olive oil
1 fat garlic clove, crushed
200g arborio rice
200ml white wine
1.2 litres hot vegetable stock
2 tbsp capers
25g plant butter
2 tbsp vegan Italian-style
cheese (optional)
1 tbsp roughly chopped dill
Salt and freshly ground
black pepper

Preheat the oven to 150°C fan/170°C/gas mark 3.

Tip the cherry tomatoes into a medium roasting tin, add the larger tomatoes cut-side up, drizzle with the extra virgin olive oil, scatter with chilli flakes, if using, tuck the thyme sprig among the tomatoes and season well with salt and freshly ground black pepper. Roast in the oven for about 30 minutes until the tomatoes are soft and starting to brown at the edges.

Meanwhile, start cooking the risotto. Combine the onion and fennel in a large sauté pan or saucepan. Add 1 tbsp of the olive oil and the garlic and cook over low-medium heat, stirring frequently for about 10 minutes until soft but not coloured.

Add the rice to the pan, stir and cook for a further minute. Add the wine and cook, stirring, until it has been absorbed by the rice. Start adding hot stock a ladleful at a time, stirring almost continuously, until each addition of stock has been absorbed by the rice.

Continue adding stock and stirring until the rice is tender and the risotto unctuous. Season well with salt and freshly ground black pepper.

Meanwhile, heat the remaining olive oil in a small frying pan over a medium heat, add the capers and fry until crisp. Drain on kitchen paper and set aside.

Stir half the roasted tomatoes through the risotto. Add the plant butter and vegan Italian-style cheese, if using, and divide the risotto between four plates. Top with the remaining roasted tomatoes and any juices from the roasting tin. Scatter with the capers and dill and serve immediately.

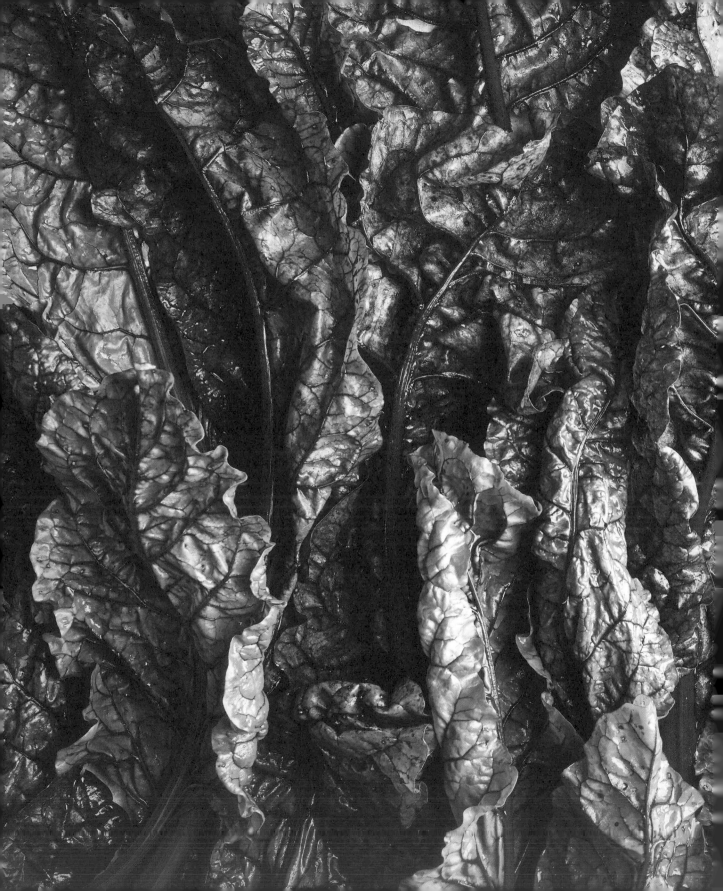

THAI CURRY WITH POTATOES AND SPINACH

The paste for this curry can be prepared in advance and stored in an airtight container in the fridge until ready to cook. Once you've made the paste, the curry comes together in no time. You can vary the veggies depending on your tastes and the season — add a handful of asparagus spears, halved Brussels sprouts, kale or fine green beans.

SERVES 4—6

PASTE
Seeds from 4 cardamom
   pods
1 tsp cumin seeds
2 whole cloves
1 tsp crushed dried
   chilli flakes
6 black peppercorns
1 tbsp sunflower oil
25g roasted cashews, plus
   extra to garnish
3 large garlic cloves,
   roughly chopped
1 fresh red chilli, deseeded
4 lime leaves
4cm piece fresh ginger
   or galangal, peeled and
   roughly chopped
2 stalks lemongrass,
   trimmed and roughly
   chopped
1 tbsp vegan fish sauce
1 tbsp soft brown or palm
   sugar, plus extra to taste

Start by making the paste. Tip the cardamom and cumin seeds, cloves, chilli flakes and peppercorns into a small frying pan and toast over a medium heat for about 1 minute until the spices smell aromatic. Grind using a pestle and mortar or spice grinder.

Tip the spice mixture into a small food processor, add the rest of the ingredients and blend to a paste.

To make the curry, heat the sunflower oil in a large sauté pan, add the onion and cook over a medium heat for about 5 minutes until tender. Add the bird's eye chilli to the pan along with the curry paste, stir well to combine and cook for a further minute or so.

Add the diced potato and sweet potato to the pan and stir to coat in the spice mixture. Pour in the coconut milk and stock, add the lime leaves and bring slowly to the boil. Reduce the heat and simmer very gently for about 20 minutes or until the potatoes are tender when tested with the point of a knife.

CURRY

1 tbsp sunflower oil

1 large onion, sliced

1 bird's eye chilli, thinly
  sliced, plus extra to
  garnish

2 potatoes (roughly 300g),
  peeled and diced

2 sweet potatoes (roughly
  600g), peeled and diced

400ml coconut milk

400ml vegetable stock

2 lime leaves

12 cherry tomatoes

6 baby corn, halved

sugar, to taste

2–3 tsp soy sauce, to taste

Juice of ½ lime, to taste

100g sugar snaps

75g young leaf spinach,
  washed

Thai basil and coriander
  leaves, to garnish

Steamed jasmine rice,
  to serve

Add the cherry tomatoes and baby corn and cook for a further 2–3 minutes to soften slightly. Taste and add a little sugar, soy sauce or lime juice to balance the sauce. Add the sugar snaps and spinach and cook until the spinach just wilts.

Spoon the curry into bowls, garnish with Thai basil and coriander leaves, extra chopped cashews and sliced chillies and serve with steamed jasmine rice.

ROOT VEGGIE PIE

SERVES 8

PASTRY

400g plain flour, plus extra
   for rolling
½ tsp cayenne pepper
200g plant-based butter,
   chilled and diced
5 tbsp ice-cold water
1 tsp white wine or
   cider vinegar

PIE FILLING

2 onions, sliced
1 leek, trimmed and sliced
2 tbsp olive oil
2 garlic cloves, sliced
1 bushy sprig of thyme,
   leaves stripped
1 bushy sprig of sage, leaves
   stripped and shredded
500g (roughly 2 medium)
   potatoes, peeled
150g (about ½ medium)
   celeriac, prepped weight
150g (about ½ medium)
   swede, prepped weight
600ml vegetable stock
25g plant-based butter
2 tsp smoked garlic paste
25g plain flour
150ml oat milk, plus extra
   for glazing
1 tbsp nutritional yeast
1 tbsp Dijon mustard
2 tbsp chopped flat-leaf
   parsley
Salt and freshly ground
   black pepper

*Everyone loves a good pie and this one is packed full of garlicky root veggies.
It's perfect for Sunday lunch or can be cooled and taken on a picnic. If you like,
add a little grated plant-based cheese to the cool filling but bear in mind that
it can be very runny when melted.*

You will need a pie dish with a base measurement of 20cm.

Start by making the pastry. Tip the flour into a bowl and add a pinch of salt
and the cayenne. Add 200g chilled diced butter and use a round-bladed
knife or palette knife to cut the butter into the flour until the pieces are
half their original size. Continue to rub the butter into the flour with your
fingertips until only very small flecks remain.

Add the ice-cold water and vinegar and combine with a round-bladed knife
until the pastry starts to clump together. Gather the pastry into a ball and
knead very lightly by hand for 10 seconds until smooth. Flatten into a disc,
cover and chill for at least 2 hours before using.

Meanwhile, prepare the filling. Tip the onions and leeks into a large, deep
frying pan, add the oil and cook over a medium heat, stirring often, for about
8 minutes until tender and only just starting to turn golden at the edges. Add
the garlic, thyme and sage, season well, cook for a further 2 minutes then
remove from the pan and set aside.

Cut the root veg into 2mm-thick slices, tip into the pan and pour over the
stock. Cover the pan with a disc of baking paper and cook over a low heat
until the veggies are tender but not falling apart when tested with the point
of a knife. Pour the contents of the pan through a colander set over a large
bowl to catch the stock (you should get 300–400ml).

Return the pan to the heat, add the butter and melt over a low–medium heat.
Add the garlic paste and cook for 30 seconds before adding the flour, stir and
cook for 30 seconds–1 minute. Pour in the oat milk and the drained vegetable
stock, whisk until smooth, bring to the boil and simmer for a further minute
to cook out the flour and thicken the sauce. Add the nutritional yeast, mustard
and parsley and season well with salt and freshly ground black pepper.

continues overleaf

Return all the root vegetables to the pan, mix to combine then remove from the heat and leave until completely cold.

Lightly dust the work surface with flour and cut the pastry into two portions, one slightly larger than the other. Roll out the larger piece into a neat disc with a thickness of 2–3mm and line the pie dish, allowing the excess pastry to hang over the edge. Spoon the filling into the pastry shell and brush the rim with a little water.

Roll out the remaining pastry into a circle just larger than the dish and carefully lift onto the pie. Press the edges together to seal and use a sharp knife to trim the excess pastry. Crimp the edges between your thumb and finger. Roll out the pastry trimmings and cut leaf shapes to decorate the top.

Glaze the surface of the pie with oat milk and chill for 20 minutes while you preheat the oven to 170°C fan/190°C/gas mark 5. At the same time, place a heavy baking tray on the middle shelf to heat up.

Cook the pie on the baking tray for about 1 hour, rotating halfway through, until the pastry is crisp and golden.

Leave the pie to rest for 10 minutes before cutting into wedges to serve.

ROOT VEGETABLE TIAN

Tian is a layered vegetable dish from Provence and the name refers to the earthenware dish in which it is cooked as much as the food itself. Tian is usually a combination of thinly sliced aubergines, tomatoes and courgettes arranged in layers and baked with herbs and generous quantities of olive oil, sometimes topped with breadcrumbs. In this recipe root vegetables are the star. They should be sliced using a mandolin or sharp knife — watch your fingers — and of similar circumference for a neater finish and even cooking time.

SERVES 4–6

2 leeks, trimmed and sliced

2 onions, thinly sliced

2 tbsp olive oil, plus extra
   for greasing

2 fat garlic cloves, crushed

1 bushy sprig of thyme,
   leaves chopped

1 bushy sprig of rosemary,
   leaves chopped

400g can of cannellini
   beans, butter beans or
   chickpeas, rinsed and
   drained

1 heaped tbsp tahini

Juice of ½ lemon

500g parsnips

1 sweet potato (roughly 350g)

2 potatoes (roughly
   300g total)

3 beetroots (roughly the size
   of a small orange)

4–6 bay leaves

2 tbsp extra virgin olive oil

200ml vegetable stock

1 tbsp breadcrumbs

1 tbsp nutritional yeast

Salt and freshly ground
   black pepper

Tip the leeks and onions into a large frying pan, add the olive oil and sweat over a low–medium heat, stirring often, for about 10 minutes until soft. Add the garlic, thyme and rosemary and season well with salt and freshly ground black pepper.

Tip half the leek and onion mixture into a food processor, add the drained beans, tahini and lemon juice and whizz until nearly smooth. Return the purée to the frying pan and combine with the remaining leeks and onions. Spoon the mixture into the bottom of a greased ovenproof dish, spread level and set aside.

Preheat the oven to 160°C fan/180°C/gas mark 4.

Peel the parsnips, sweet potato, potatoes and beetroot and using a sharp knife or mandolin cut each vegetable into 2mm-thick discs. Keep each vegetable separate and stacked neatly.

Starting at one side of the dish stack 3 slices of parsnip on top of the bean mixture, positioning the slices almost vertically. Follow with 3 slices of sweet potato, then potato and then beetroot. Continue layering the veg to fill the dish, neatly and tightly packed and either in rows if your dish is rectangular or in concentric circles if it is round.

continues overleaf

Tuck the bay leaves in among the veggies, season well with salt and freshly ground black pepper and drizzle with 1 tbsp of the extra virgin olive oil. Pour the stock over the top, cover the dish tightly with foil and bake on the middle shelf of the oven for 1 hour. Remove the foil and cook for 30 minutes more.

In a small bowl combine the breadcrumbs and nutritional yeast. Scatter over the top of the tian, drizzle with the remaining extra virgin olive oil and bake for a further 10 minutes or until the vegetables are tender when tested with a skewer or the point of a knife and are starting to brown and crisp at the edges. The final cooking time will depend on how thick the vegetables are sliced and how densely they are packed into the dish.

Leave to cool and settle for 5 minutes before serving.

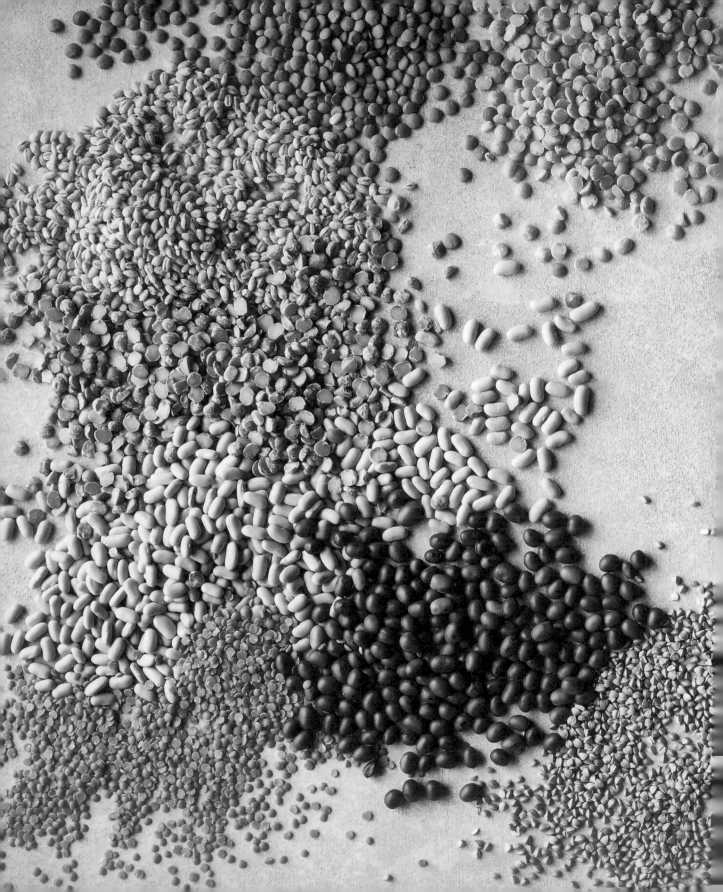

SOUPS & LIGHT BITES

SUMMER MINESTRONE

SERVES 6

200g fresh borlotti beans
  (podded weight)
3 garlic cloves
2 bay leaves
1 onion, finely chopped
1 small fennel bulb, cut into
  1cm dice, feathery fronds
  reserved
2 carrots, diced
2 small celery sticks, diced
1 small leek, trimmed
  and diced
2 tbsp olive oil
½ tsp fennel seeds
1 litre vegetable stock
1 green courgette, trimmed
  and diced
1 yellow courgette, trimmed
  and diced
100g green beans, trimmed
  and chopped small
1 small bunch of basil, leaves
  picked
1 sprig of oregano
2 courgette flowers
  (optional)
Salt and freshly ground
  black pepper

TO SERVE
8 slices of ciabatta,
  sourdough or focaccia
1 garlic clove, cut in half
Green olive tapenade
Fruity extra virgin olive oil,
  for drizzling

This soup is a wonderful example of making the most of the seasonal best. If you can find or grow fresh borlotti beans do use them in this soup — not only are the raw beans pretty but the taste is far better than tinned. Freshly podded broad beans or peas make perfectly good substitutes and a handful of shredded kale, cavolo nero or spinach would be worthwhile additions. If you are growing courgettes and have flowers to spare they can be roughly chopped and added along with the fresh herbs.

Start by cooking the borlotti beans. Tip the podded beans into a small pan, add 1 whole garlic clove and a bay leaf, cover with water and simmer for 20–30 minutes or until tender.

Meanwhile, tip the onion, fennel, carrot, celery and leek into a large saucepan. Add the olive oil and cook over a medium heat for about 10 minutes, stirring often, until softened but not browned.

Crush the remaining garlic, add to the pan with the fennel seeds and cook for a further minute. Pour the stock into the pan, add the drained borlotti beans and 1 bay leaf, season well and bring to the boil. Reduce to a gentle simmer for about 25 minutes until the vegetables are tender.

Add the courgettes and green beans and add to the soup. Roughly chop the basil and oregano leaves and courgette flowers (if using), add to the pan and cook for a further 3–4 minutes until the green veggies are tender. Taste and add seasoning if needed.

Toast the bread, rub with the garlic halves and top with the green olive tapenade. Spoon the minestrone into bowls, drizzle with fruity olive oil and serve with green olive toasts on the side.

PUMPKIN SOUP WITH CHESTNUTS

For this soup you will need to roast the pumpkin, cut into wedges, first to intensify its sweet flavour, which marries perfectly with the nutty earthiness of cooked chestnuts and sage. Pumpkins cooked in this way are also delicious served with soft polenta, stirred through risotto or as a filling for pasta.

SERVES 6–8

1 medium Hokkaido
   pumpkin, cut into 3cm-
   thick wedges, seeds and
   fibre removed
3 fat garlic cloves, unpeeled
2 sprigs of sage
4 tbsp olive oil
1 large onion, diced
1 small leek, trimmed and
   chopped small
2 carrots, diced
1 bay leaf
1 medium floury
   potato, diced
120g cooked chestnuts
1 litre vegetable stock

TO SERVE

2 tbsp pumpkin seeds
2 cooked chestnuts, roughly
   crumbled
8–12 sage leaves
2 tbsp oat crème fraîche
Salt and freshly ground
   black pepper

Preheat the oven to 160°C fan/180°C/gas mark 4.

Arrange the pumpkin in a roasting tin, tucking in the whole garlic cloves and sprigs of sage between the wedges. Season, drizzle with 1 tbsp olive oil and loosely cover the tin with foil. Roast the squash for about 40 minutes or until tender when tested with the point of a knife.

Meanwhile, tip the onion, leek and carrots into a large saucepan. Add the bay leaf and 1 tbsp olive oil and cook over a low–medium heat for about 10 minutes, stirring frequently, until the vegetables are tender but not coloured.

Use a spoon or knife to scoop the soft pumpkin flesh into the pan, discarding the skin. Squeeze the garlic cloves from their skins and add to the pan with the potato and chestnuts. Add the stock, season well and simmer for about 20 minutes until the potato is soft when tested with the point of a knife.

Meanwhile, toast the pumpkin seeds and crumbled chestnuts in a dry frying pan over a medium heat for about 1 minute until the seeds start to pop. Remove from the pan. Heat the remaining 2 tbsp olive oil in the frying pan and fry the sage leaves until crisp. Drain on kitchen paper.

Pick out the bay leaf and blend the soup until smooth using a stick blender. Taste and add more salt and pepper as required.

Ladle the soup into bowls. Serve with a swirl of crème fraîche and topped with the pumpkin seeds, chestnuts and crisp sage leaves.

HOT AND SOUR BUTTERNUT SQUASH SOUP

This is a wonderful warming soup with a hit of hot chilli, sourness from tamarind and lime, tempered with a cooling swirl of coconut milk and vibrant Thai basil oil.

SERVES 4–6

1 large onion, chopped

5 tbsp sunflower oil

1 large stalk lemongrass

2 fat garlic cloves, finely chopped

4cm piece fresh ginger, finely chopped

1 bird's eye chilli, finely chopped (include the seeds if you like it hot)

1 medium butternut squash, peeled, deseeded and cut into large dice (about 650g prepped weight)

2 lime leaves

800ml vegetable stock

200ml full fat coconut milk, plus extra to serve

1 tbsp tamarind paste

1 small bunch of Thai basil, leaves picked

4 small or 2 large shallots, thinly sliced

Juice of ½ lime

2–3 tsp soy sauce

Salt and freshly ground black pepper

Tip the onion into a large saucepan, add 1 tbsp of the sunflower oil and cook over a low–medium heat, stirring often, until the onion is soft but not coloured. Bash the lemongrass two or three times with a rolling pin to break the fibres. Add it to the pan with the garlic, ginger and chilli, mix to combine and cook for a further 2 minutes until fragrant. Add the diced squash and lime leaves, season well with salt and freshly ground black pepper, stir to coat in the mixture then add the stock, coconut milk and tamarind paste. Slowly bring the soup to the boil, reduce the heat to a gentle simmer and cook for about 30 minutes or until the squash is really tender.

Meanwhile, tip half the Thai basil leaves into a small blender or food processor, add 3 tbsp of the sunflower oil and blend until smooth. Chill until ready to use. Fry the shallots in the remaining oil in a small frying pan over a medium heat, stirring frequently for about 5 minutes until golden and crisp. Drain on kitchen paper.

Remove the lime leaves and lemongrass stalk from the soup and blend until smooth. Add lime juice and soy sauce, taste and add salt and freshly ground black pepper if needed.

Ladle the soup into bowls, drizzle over a little coconut milk and Thai basil oil, and serve scattered with crisp shallots and Thai basil leaves.

MEXICAN TOMATO SOUP
WITH AVOCADO SALSA AND FRIED TORTILLAS

SERVES 6

2 small onions, finely chopped
2 tbsp olive oil
2 garlic cloves, finely chopped
1 green chilli, finely chopped
2–3 tsp chipotle paste
1 tsp cumin seeds
1 tsp dried oregano
2 roasted red peppers,
    drained, deseeded and
    roughly chopped
350g fresh tomatoes, cored
    and roughly chopped
1 x 400g can of chopped
    tomatoes
500ml vegetable stock
2 bay leaves
1 tsp sugar
1–2 tsp red wine vinegar
Salt and freshly ground
    black pepper
150g buckwheat

SALSA

1 avocado, halved, stoned
    and diced
½ red onion, diced
2 tbsp cooked black-eyed
    beans
8 cherry tomatoes, quartered
Juice of ½ lime

FRIED TORTILLAS

2 flour tortillas
3 tbsp sunflower oil

TO SERVE

2 tbsp chopped coriander
1½ limes, cut into 6 wedges

This soup is a meal in itself — the warming, chilli-spiked tomato soup is poured over cooked buckwheat, topped with a fresh tomato and bean salsa and served with fried tortilla triangles. You can swap the buckwheat for brown rice if you prefer and the fried flour tortillas for bought tortilla chips.

Tip the onions into a large saucepan, add the olive oil and cook over a low– medium heat for 8–10 minutes, stirring frequently, until softened. Add the garlic and chilli to the pan with the chipotle paste, cumin seeds and oregano. Stir to combine and cook for a further minute.

Add the roasted peppers to the pan with the fresh and tinned tomatoes. Continue cooking for a further 2–3 minutes before adding the stock, bay leaves and sugar. Season well with salt and freshly ground black pepper.

Bring to the boil, reduce the heat to a gentle simmer and cook for about 30 minutes until the tomatoes are very soft. Remove the bay leaves and blend the soup until smooth, taste and add a dash of sugar, vinegar or salt and pepper as needed.

Meanwhile, bring a pan of salted water to the boil. Toast the buckwheat in a dry frying pan for 1 minute, stirring constantly. Remove from the heat and tip into the pan of boiling water for about 20 minutes or until tender. Drain and keep warm. You will need the frying pan for the tortillas, so keep it handy.

Prepare the salsa. Tip the avocado and red onion into a bowl and add the cooked black-eyed beans. Add the cherry tomatoes to the mixture with the lime juice and season well with salt and freshly ground black pepper.

Cut the tortillas into small triangles or strips. Fry in the sunflower oil until crisp and golden. Drain on kitchen paper.

Divide the warm buckwheat between 6 bowls and ladle over the soup. Serve with the avocado salsa, fried tortilla chips, coriander leaves and the lime wedges for squeezing over.

MUSHROOM BROTH WITH BUCKWHEAT SOBA

SERVES 4

BROTH

150g oyster mushrooms, roughly torn in half

130g shiitake mushrooms, roughly torn in half

2 tsp sunflower oil

10g dried shiitake mushrooms

2 spring onions, trimmed and halved

1 garlic clove, sliced

3cm piece fresh ginger, peeled and sliced

2 star anise

½ tsp coriander seeds

SOBA

200g buckwheat soba noodles

6 shiitake mushrooms, trimmed and sliced

1 tbsp soy sauce or tamari, to taste

1 tsp mirin or rice vinegar, to taste

3 baby pak choi, halved or quartered

Salt and freshly ground black pepper

TO SERVE

2 spring onions, trimmed and finely shredded

Shichimi togarashi or toasted sesame seeds

This light broth has plenty of satisfying umami notes. Mushrooms are roasted then simmered with aromatics to create a rich stock. Prepare this broth ahead of serving to allow plenty of time for the flavours to shine through.

Preheat the oven to 160°C fan/180°C/gas mark 4.

First make the broth. Toss the torn oyster and shiitake mushrooms in the sunflower oil and season. Tip onto a large baking tray in a single layer and roast for about 30 minutes, turning halfway through until browned and starting to crisp at the edges.

Scoop the roasted mushrooms into a large saucepan and add the rest of the broth ingredients. Add 750ml water and bring slowly to the boil. Reduce the heat to a simmer and cook over a low heat for about 30 minutes to extract as much flavour as possible from the mushrooms and aromatics. Remove from the heat and leave to cool to room temperature or chill until ready to serve.

Cook the buckwheat noodles according to the packet instructions. Drain and divide between 4 bowls. While the noodles are cooking strain the cooled broth through a sieve into a clean pan, pressing down on the mushrooms to extract as much flavour as possible. Bring the stock to a simmer, add the sliced shiitake mushrooms and cook for 2–3 minutes until tender. Taste the broth and add soy sauce and mirin to taste. Add the pak choi to the broth and cook for a further minute until tender.

Ladle the broth over the buckwheat noodles, dividing the mushrooms and pak choi evenly between the bowls, and scatter with spring onions and shichimi togarashi or sesame seeds to serve.

PEARL BARLEY AND CAVOLO NERO BROTH

This soup is perfect for a hearty lunch with a thick slice of sourdough bread. If not being eaten immediately, the barley will continue to swell, so you may need to add more stock on reheating.

SERVES 4—6

1 large onion, cut into
  1cm dice
1 leek, trimmed and cut into
  1cm dice
2 carrots, cut into 1cm dice
1 small fennel bulb or
  2 celery sticks, trimmed
  and cut into 1cm dice
2 tbsp olive oil
2 fat garlic cloves, crushed
1 bay leaf
1 sprig of thyme
2 large sprigs of flat-leaf
  parsley
1.2–1.4 litres vegetable stock
100g pearl barley, rinsed
  and drained
100g cavolo nero, central
  rib removed and leaves
  shredded
2 tbsp extra virgin olive oil
Salt and freshly ground
  black pepper

Tip the onion, leek, carrot and fennel into a large saucepan and stir to combine. Add the olive oil and cook over a low–medium heat, stirring frequently, for 8–10 minutes until just starting to soften. Add the garlic and cook for a further minute.

While the veggies are cooking tie the bay leaf, thyme sprigs and parsley stalks into a little bundle with kitchen string. Chop the parsley leaves for garnish, cover and chill until needed.

Pour 1.2 litres stock into the saucepan, add the herb bundle and bring slowly to the boil. Add the pearl barley to the soup and season well with salt and freshly ground black pepper. Cook for about 30 minutes until the pearl barley is tender, adding a little more stock if the soup is too thick.

Remove the herb bundle from the pot, add the shredded cavolo nero, mix to combine and cook for a further minute or so until wilted.

Ladle the broth into bowls, drizzle with a little extra virgin olive oil and scatter with chopped parsley to serve.

POTSTICKERS

MAKES 24

10g dried shiitake
  mushrooms
3 tbsp sunflower oil
1 fat garlic clove, crushed
4cm piece fresh ginger,
  finely grated
1 red chilli, deseeded and
  finely chopped
3 spring onions, trimmed
  and finely sliced, plus
  extra to garnish
100g fresh shiitake
  mushrooms, trimmed
  and finely chopped
1 carrot, finely diced
100g Chinese leaf, spring
  greens or Savoy cabbage,
  tough parts removed and
  leaves finely shredded
100g broccoli, finely
  chopped
50g sliced water chestnuts,
  chopped
2 tbsp chopped coriander
3 tsp soy sauce
A dash of sesame oil
A pinch of ground white
  pepper
24 gyoza skins or wrappers

DIPPING SAUCE

4cm piece fresh ginger, cut
  into fine julienne strips
2 tsp chilli oil
2 tbsp soy sauce
2 tbsp black vinegar
2 tsp rice vinegar

Universally popular and almost impossible to resist, these tasty little dumplings, known to the Chinese as potstickers and to the Japanese as gyoza, are jam-packed with crisp vegetables and served with a dipping sauce spiked with ginger and chilli. Gyoza skins or wrappers are readily available in Asian supermarkets or online. Filling the dumplings can take a little practice if you want them perfectly pleated.

Soak the dried shiitake in a small bowl of just-boiled water for 15 minutes.

Heat 1 tbsp of the sunflower oil in a large frying pan or wok over a medium heat and add the garlic, ginger, chilli and sliced spring onions and cook, stirring constantly, for 1 minute.

Drain the rehydrated shiitake, pat dry on kitchen paper and finely chop. Add to the pan with the fresh mushrooms and carrot and cook for 2 minutes until starting to soften. Add the cabbage, broccoli and water chestnuts, stir-fry for a further minute then add the coriander, soy sauce, sesame oil and white pepper. Mix to combine then remove from the heat and leave to cool to room temperature.

Meanwhile, prepare the dipping sauce. Put the ginger in a bowl. Pour over the chilli oil, soy sauce, black and rice vinegars and mix. Cover and set aside.

Working in batches, lay 6 dumpling wrappers on the work surface and place a neat dessertspoonful of filling in the middle of each. Brush the edges with cold water, fold over and pinch together to seal the filling into a half-moon shaped dumpling. Place the filled dumplings on a tray and cover while you fill the remaining wrappers.

Heat 1 tbsp sunflower oil in a large frying pan over a medium heat, add half the dumplings and cook over a medium heat for 2–3 minutes until the underside is golden brown. Add 3–4 tbsp water to the pan, immediately cover with a lid and continue to cook for a further minute.

Remove from the pan, heat the remaining tablespoon of oil and cook the rest of the dumplings in the same way. Serve with the dipping sauce.

BEETROOT AND SPINACH FALAFEL

MAKES 20/SERVES 4–6

200g dried chickpeas,
  soaked overnight in a large
  bowl of cold water
1 onion, chopped
1 tbsp olive oil
250g raw beetroot (about
  2 tennis-ball size beets)
2 fat garlic cloves, crushed
1 tsp ground cumin
½ tsp cayenne pepper
100g young leaf spinach,
  washed
100g fresh breadcrumbs
2 tbsp tahini
50g pine kernels, toasted
Juice of ½ lemon
50g sesame seeds
About 6 tbsp sunflower oil
Salt and freshly ground
  black pepper

YOGURT DIP

250ml dairy-free yogurt
1 tbsp tahini
1 tbsp finely chopped dill
1 tbsp finely chopped flat-
  leaf parsley
1 garlic clove, crushed
1 tsp ground sumac
Juice of ½ lemon

TO SERVE

Quick Flatbreads, warmed
  (see page 158)
Pickled chillies or pickled
  red onions
Small cucumbers, cut into
  long wedges

Adding beetroot and spinach to falafel is a good way to boost your veggie intake but is far from what is an authentic falafel – apologies to the purists, but they are delicious! For this recipe you need to soak the dried chickpeas the day before you intend to cook the falafel, so plan accordingly.

Drain the soaked chickpeas and rinse under cold running water. Set aside.

Tip the onion into a large frying pan, add the olive oil and cook, stirring often, over a medium heat for about 8 minutes until tender but not coloured. Meanwhile, peel and coarsely grate the beetroot. If your beets still have the stems and leaves attached, chop those too and keep them separate. Lay the grated beetroot on a double thickness of kitchen paper to absorb any excess moisture.

Add the garlic, cumin and cayenne to the onions and cook for a further minute or so before adding the grated beetroot. Cook, stirring frequently, for about 2 minutes until the beetroot dries out and softens a little. Add the spinach (and any chopped beetroot leaves and stalks) to the pan and cook quickly for another minute until the leaves are wilted and any moisture has been cooked off.

Tip the drained chickpeas into a food processor. Add the breadcrumbs and tahini and blend until thoroughly combined but not quite smooth; the chickpeas should still have some texture. Add the contents of the frying pan, the pine kernels and lemon juice and season well with salt and freshly ground black pepper. Blend again until the mixture starts to clump together.

Transfer the mixture to a bowl, taste and add more seasoning if needed. Using your hands, shape the mixture into 20 balls (golf-ball size) and flatten into patties. Press sesame seeds into the top and underside of each one.

Wipe out the frying pan, heat 3 tbsp of the sunflower oil over a medium heat and cook the falafel, in batches, until crisp and browned on both sides.

Meanwhile, make the dip. Combine the yogurt, tahini, chopped herbs, garlic, sumac and lemon juice in a bowl and season well.

Serve the falafel with the yogurt dip, warm flatbreads, pickled chillies or red onions and cucumber wedges.

CHARGRILLED COURGETTES WITH CANNELLINI BEAN PURÉE
AND LEMON AND HERB DRESSING

For this recipe you will need to soak the dried cannellini beans overnight but it's worth it. Dried beans are not only cheaper than the tinned ones, they take up less cupboard space, use less packaging and are far superior in taste. You can switch the hazelnuts for almonds or even mixed seeds if you prefer and the oregano for thyme, dill or mint. Grating the lemon directly over the salad means that the wonderful oils from the zest are not lost to the air but add extra flavour to this simple but delicious dish.

SERVES 4 AS A LIGHT STARTER

100g dried cannellini beans, soaked in a large bowl of cold water overnight
1 bay leaf
1 garlic clove
5 tbsp extra virgin olive oil
1 unwaxed lemon, zest of half and juice of all
3 courgettes, trimmed
30g pistachios or toasted hazelnuts, roughly chopped
1 tbsp fresh oregano leaves
1 tbsp roughly chopped flat-leaf parsley
4 slices of sourdough bread or focaccia
Salt and freshly ground black pepper

Drain and rinse the soaked beans, tip into a medium saucepan, add the bay leaf and the whole garlic clove and cover with fresh water. Bring to the boil, reduce to a simmer and cook for about 40 minutes or until the beans are tender. Remove from the heat and leave the beans to cool to room temperature in the cooking water.

Remove the bay leaf, drain the beans and tip into a food processor with the garlic clove. Whizz until nearly smooth, scraping down the sides of the bowl, and season well with salt and freshly ground black pepper. With the motor running add 2 tbsp of the olive oil and the juice of ½ the lemon to make a smooth purée. Taste and add more seasoning or lemon juice if needed. Spoon into a shallow serving dish and cover until needed.

Cut the courgettes in half across their middles. Slice each half lengthways into four wedges. Tip into a bowl, drizzle with 1 tbsp olive oil and season. Heat a ridged griddle pan over a medium heat. Add the courgettes and cook on all sides until nicely charred and just starting to soften. You may need to cook the courgettes in batches, depending on the size of your griddle pan.

Arrange the courgettes on top of the bean purée and scatter with the chopped pistachios and oregano leaves. Grate the zest of the remaining lemon half directly over the salad and squeeze 1 tbsp of the juice into a bowl. Stir in the remaining 2 tbsp olive oil, the chopped parsley and some seasoning, then spoon the dressing over the courgettes.

Toast the sourdough on the griddle pan and serve alongside the salad.

CHINESE SPRING ONION PANCAKES

These crispy, flaky pancakes, known as Cong You Bing, are a delicious snack or appetizer with a salty soy dipping sauce. The trick to getting crisp layers and a slightly chewy middle is not to flatten each pancake too much and to fry them over a medium heat, flipping the pancakes from time to time until golden. Sesame seeds in the filling are not an authentic addition to this Chinese staple but a delicious one nonetheless. Black vinegar, which you can find in Chinese supermarkets, is a form of rice vinegar that is malted and aged for a richer flavour.

MAKES/SERVES 6

250g plain flour, plus 2 tbsp, and extra for rolling
½ tsp salt
½ tsp Chinese five-spice
160–175ml boiling water
2 tbsp toasted sesame oil
6–8 spring onions, trimmed, halved lengthways and thinly sliced
2 tsp sesame seeds, toasted
1 tbsp sunflower oil

DIPPING SAUCE

2 tbsp soy sauce
1 tbsp black vinegar
2 tsp tahini
2 tsp chilli oil

Combine 250g flour, the salt and five-spice in a mixing bowl. Add 160ml water, mixing with chopsticks or a fork until the dough starts to come together. It should be soft but not sticky; only add more water if needed. Continue mixing with your hands until the dough is smooth. Turn onto a clean work surface and knead for about 3 minutes until the dough is silky smooth. Shape into a ball, return to the bowl, cover with a clean tea towel and leave the dough to rest for 30 minutes at room temperature.

Meanwhile, make the dipping sauce. Combine all the ingredients in a small bowl, mix until smooth and add a teaspoon or two of cold water to loosen. Set aside.

In a separate small bowl combine the sesame oil with the remaining 2 tbsp flour and mix until smooth. Lightly dust the work surface with flour and roll the dough out into a neat rectangle measuring 30 x 40cm and with one of the shorter sides nearest you. Brush the sesame oil mixture evenly over the surface of the dough and scatter with the chopped spring onions and sesame seeds. Starting at the bottom edge and working away from you, roll the dough into a neat, tight log encasing the spring onions.

continues overleaf

Cut the log into six even-sized rolls. Lightly dust the work surface with flour and stand one of the rolls upright on the work surface. Using the palm of your hand flatten the cylinder onto the work surface then, using the rolling pin, roll the pancake into a 15cm disc, rolling from the middle to the edge of the pancake and rotating the pancake as you do so. You want to slightly open the layers without entirely flattening them.

Heat the sunflower oil in a large frying pan over a medium heat. Add the pancake and cook for about 3 minutes on each side until crisp and golden brown. While it cooks roll out the next one and continue until you have made all six. Keep the pancakes warm in a moderate oven while you cook the remainder.

Serve warm, cut into wedges, with the dipping sauce.

CAULIFLOWER BUFFALO WINGS

*Hot, spicy, crispy bite-size pieces of cauliflower with a cooling avocado dip —
what's not to like? Perfect as a starter for a barbecue or as nibbles with something
cold and refreshing…*

SERVES 4–6

BUFFALO WINGS
150g plain flour
½ tsp smoked paprika
½ tsp onion granules
½ tsp garlic granules
½ tsp dried oregano
200–225ml dairy-free milk
1 cauliflower, trimmed and
   cut into bite-size florets
150g panko breadcrumbs
Lime wedges, to serve

HOT SAUCE
100g plant butter
200ml hot sauce
2 tbsp maple or agave syrup
Juice of 1 lime
4 tsp soy sauce

AVOCADO JALAPEÑO DIP
2 ripe avocados
3 tbsp dairy-free yogurt
1 large garlic clove, crushed
1 heaped tbsp jalapeño
   slices, drained
Juice of 1 lime
2 tbsp chopped coriander,
   plus extra to garnish
Salt and freshly ground
   black pepper

Preheat the oven to 170°C fan/190°C/gas 5 and line a large baking tray with baking paper.

In a large mixing bowl combine the flour, paprika, onion and garlic granules and dried oregano and season well with salt and freshly ground black pepper. Add the milk and whisk to form a thick, coating batter. If it's a little thick add a drop more milk or water or, if it's too thin, add a little more flour.

Tip the panko crumbs into another large bowl. Put all the cauliflower florets into the batter and use your hands to coat each piece thoroughly. Add a quarter of the batter-coated florets to the breadcrumbs and toss to coat. Place the crumb-coated florets on the lined baking tray and continue to coat the remaining cauliflower, in batches, and place on the baking tray.

Bake the cauliflower for 30 minutes until the breadcrumb coating is crisp and the cauliflower tender.

Meanwhile, prepare the hot sauce. Melt the plant butter in a small pan, add the hot sauce, maple syrup, lime juice and soy sauce and combine.

Remove the cauliflower from the oven, spoon the sauce over and turn the pieces over on the tray to coat. Return to the oven for a further 10–12 minutes to crisp.

To make the dip, halve and stone the avocados and scoop the flesh into a food processor. Add the rest of the ingredients, season and blend until smooth. Spoon into a bowl.

Serve the crisp cauliflower on a sharing plate with the avocado dip and lime wedges for squeezing over.

TENDERSTEM, KALE AND COURGETTE PAKORA
WITH GREEN CHILLI, CORIANDER AND LIME DIP

MAKES 14–16/SERVES 4–6

1 large courgette, trimmed and coarsely grated or julienned

100g tenderstem broccoli, stalks finely sliced and leafy tops roughly chopped

75g kale, central stalk removed, leaves finely shredded

1 onion, thinly sliced

1 large garlic clove, crushed

3cm piece fresh ginger, grated

1 bird's eye chilli, finely chopped

225g gram flour

½ tsp cumin seeds

½ tsp nigella seeds

½ tsp ground turmeric

½ tsp chilli powder

175ml cold water

700ml sunflower oil for deep-frying

Salt and freshly ground black pepper

DIPPING SAUCE

1 small bunch of fresh coriander

1 garlic clove, roughly chopped

2cm piece fresh ginger, peeled and roughly chopped

1 large green chilli, deseeded and roughly chopped

Juice of 1 lime, plus extra wedges to serve

2 tbsp plant-based yogurt

These spicy green-veg pakora are perfect to serve as an appetizer to start a curry-themed feast. They can be cooked ahead of time and reheated in a moderate oven until crisp. This trio of green vegetables can be adapted to your tastes and the season. Shredded Brussels sprouts, small cauliflower florets, sliced peppers, sweetcorn, peas and shredded carrots would all be perfect swaps.

Dry the grated or julienned courgette on kitchen paper and tip into a large mixing bowl. Add the broccoli stalks and leafy tops together with the kale, onion, garlic, ginger and chilli. Mix to combine.

In a separate bowl combine the gram flour with the spices, add the measured water, season well with salt and freshly ground black pepper and beat until smooth. Add to the prepared vegetables and mix well.

Heat the sunflower oil to 180°C in a deep pan, wok or deep-fryer.

While the oil is coming up to temperature prepare the dipping sauce. Put the coriander, garlic, ginger, green chilli and lime juice in the bowl of a small food processor and season well. Blend until very finely chopped, add the yogurt and whizz again to combine. Spoon into a bowl, cover and chill until ready to serve.

Using two tablespoons drop spoonfuls of the pakora mix into the hot oil, cooking 3–4 pakora at a time, for about 4 minutes until crisp and golden brown. Remove from the hot oil using a slotted spoon and drain well on kitchen paper. Keep warm while you fry the remaining mixture.

Serve the pakora hot or warm with the dipping sauce and fresh lime wedges to squeeze over.

SPINACH AND 'FETA' FILO PARCELS

Almost every bakery in Greece sells filo pastries filled with spinach and feta (or other local cheese). These are my vegan version of a much-loved holiday treat. Vegan Greek-style cheese is very good in salads but does not bake very well. So the answer here is to use firm tofu, which crumbles in much the same way as feta and absorbs the other flavours well. The preserved lemon, chilli and green olives all combine to give a super-savoury flavour, but if you prefer you could use freshly grated lemon zest and a mild, fresh green chilli.

MAKES 12

6 spring onions, trimmed
  and finely sliced
1 garlic clove, crushed
4 tbsp olive oil
75g young leaf spinach
1 small preserved lemon
1 pickled green chilli, finely
  chopped
12 pitted green olives,
  roughly chopped
1 small courgette, coarsely
  grated to give 75–100g
  (discard the soft centre)
125g extra firm tofu, drained
  and crumbled or cut into
  very small pieces
1 small bunch of fresh dill,
  chopped
3 tsp nutritional yeast
½ tsp ground sumac
6–8 sheets filo pastry
3 tsp sesame seeds
Salt and freshly ground
  black pepper

Preheat the oven to 170°C fan/190°C/gas mark 5.

Tip the spring onions into a large frying pan, add the garlic and 1 tbsp olive oil and cook over a medium heat for about 2 minutes, stirring frequently, until softened. Add the spinach to the pan and continue to cook for a further minute until wilted. Tip the contents of the pan into a bowl.

Cut the preserved lemon into quarters, cut away and discard the soft middle and any pips and slice the skin into fine shreds. Add to the spinach bowl, along with the chilli, olives, courgette, tofu, dill and nutritional yeast. Season well with sumac and salt and freshly ground black pepper. Mix to combine.

Lay one sheet of filo on a clean work surface and brush with olive oil. Lay a second sheet neatly on top and press the two together. With the long side of the pastry nearest you, cut the filo into strips 7–8cm wide and place a neat dessertspoon of the filling near the top right-hand corner of each strip. Lightly brush each pastry strip with oil. Fold the right-hand corner over and down to encase and cover the filling in a neat triangle. Repeat folding over and down each strip to create a neat triangular parcel. Arrange on a lined baking sheet and repeat until you have 12 parcels and have used up all the filling.

Brush the top of each parcel with a little more olive oil and scatter with sesame seeds. Bake on the middle shelf of the oven for 20 minutes until crisp and golden brown.

FARINATA WITH PEPPERS AND CHERRY TOMATOES

This delicious savoury pancake hails from Liguria and for surprisingly few ingredients, is really quite scrumptious. The roasted peppers and tomatoes take the farinata from a side dish to a main player. You will need to mix up the batter 12 hours before you intend to cook and serve, so plan in advance.

SERVES 4–6

125g gram flour

200–225ml warm water

4 tbsp extra virgin olive oil

1 tsp salt

2 small onions, chopped

2 garlic cloves, crushed

1 tsp fennel seeds

1 tsp dried oregano

1 bushy sprig of rosemary,
   leaves picked and chopped

Salt and freshly ground
   black pepper

PEPPERS AND TOMATOES

2 tbsp extra virgin olive oil

1 red pepper, quartered,
   deseeded and cut into
   1cm-thick strips

1 yellow pepper, quartered,
   deseeded and cut into
   1cm-thick strips

100g cherry tomatoes,
   halved

2 garlic cloves, crushed

2 tsp balsamic vinegar

1 tbsp chopped flat-leaf
   parsley

Combine the gram flour with 200ml warm water, 2 tbsp of the olive oil and 1 tsp salt in a mixing bowl. Whisk until smooth and the consistency of double cream, gradually adding a little more water or flour as needed. Cover and leave at room temperature overnight for 12 hours.

You can make the pepper and tomato side dish in advance. Heat the olive oil in a large frying pan over a low–medium heat, add the peppers, season well with salt and freshly ground black pepper and cook, stirring frequently, for about 30 minutes until soft. Add the cherry tomatoes and garlic and continue to cook for a further 10 minutes until the tomatoes are soft and juicy. Add the balsamic vinegar and chopped parsley and remove from the heat. Set aside until you're ready to serve the farinata.

When you're ready to cook, preheat the grill. Tip the onions into a non-stick, ovenproof 20cm sauté pan and add 2 tbsp olive oil. Cook over a medium heat, stirring frequently, for about 10 minutes until the onions are tender and starting to turn golden at the edges. Add the crushed garlic, fennel seeds, dried oregano and chopped rosemary and cook for a further 2 minutes. Remove half the onion mixture and set aside on a plate.

Season the batter with a grinding of black pepper and whisk to combine. Pour half the batter into the sauté pan, around and over the onions, and continue to cook, without stirring, for about 1 minute until the edges of the farinata start to sizzle and set and the underside is golden brown. Slide the pan under the hot grill and cook for about 2 minutes until the top of the farinata is set and golden brown. Slide out of the pan and leave to cool for a minute or so while you cook a second pancake with the reserved onions.

Cut the farinata into wedges and serve with the peppers and tomatoes, which can be at room temperature or gently reheated.

SALADS

BLACK RICE SALAD WITH COLOURFUL CHARGRILLED VEG

Black Venus rice is deliciously nutty and absorbs flavours well, making it perfect for salads with a punchy dressing. As well as being tasty it looks dramatic against the bright orange sweet potatoes and vibrant green broccoli. If you don't have a ridged griddle pan, simply roast the veggies in the hot oven — the sweet potato wedges will take about 30 minutes and the broccoli, spring onions and chilli 10.

SERVES 4

225g black Venus rice
2 small–medium sweet
   potatoes, scrubbed and cut
   lengthways into 8 wedges
2 tbsp sunflower oil
½ tsp dried chilli flakes
150g broccoli florets
6 spring onions, trimmed
1 fresh whole jalapeño or
   green chilli
2 tbsp roughly chopped
   coriander
1 tbsp roughly chopped
   flat-leaf parsley
Salt and freshly ground
   black pepper
2 tsp toasted sesame seeds,
   to serve

DRESSING
1 tbsp white miso
1 tbsp tahini
2 tsp maple or agave syrup
2 tsp grated fresh ginger
1 garlic clove, crushed
Juice of 1 lime
3 tbsp sunflower or
   rapeseed oil
2 tbsp toasted sesame oil

Preheat the oven to 180°C fan/200°C/gas mark 6.

Rinse the rice in a sieve under cold running water for 30 seconds and then cook in boiling salted water for 35–40 minutes or until tender.

Meanwhile, tip the sweet potato wedges into a large mixing bowl. Add the sunflower oil and chilli flakes and season with salt and freshly ground black pepper. Mix to coat the wedges in the oil, arrange on a large baking tray and roast in the oven for 10 minutes until starting to soften. Tip the broccoli florets into the bowl and mix to coat in any residual oil and seasoning.

Prepare the dressing. Combine the miso, tahini, maple syrup, ginger, garlic and lime juice in a bowl and whisk to combine. Add the sunflower oil, sesame oil and 1 tbsp water and whisk again until smooth.

Heat a ridged griddle pan over a medium heat. Cook the half-baked sweet potato wedges on the griddle pan for about 10 minutes, turning once or twice until tender and nicely charred. Remove to the baking tray. Tip the broccoli, whole spring onions and whole chilli onto the griddle pan and cook until tender and charred. Transfer the broccoli and spring onions to the tray with the sweet potato wedges where they can cool slightly. Trim the stalk from the green chilli and finely chop it — seeds and all.

Drain the rice, rinse under cold running water and leave to drain well in a sieve. Tip the rice into the mixing bowl, add 3 tbsp of the dressing, the chopped herbs and green chilli, season with salt and freshly ground black pepper and mix. Spoon into a serving dish, arrange the chargrilled veg on top and drizzle over more dressing. Scatter with toasted sesame seeds to serve.

FREEKEH AND QUINOA TABBOULEH

More often than not tabbouleh is made with bulgur wheat, and usually consists of more herbs than grains. In this recipe freekeh and quinoa replace bulgur wheat for a salad with a distinct nuttiness. Freekeh are young wholewheat grains which are dried and lightly toasted — delicious in salads or served warm as an alternative to rice. The quinoa adds another layer of texture.

SERVES 4

100g wholegrain freekeh, rinsed under cold running water

50g quinoa, rinsed under cold running water

2 tbsp olive oil

1 aubergine, trimmed and cut into 1–2cm dice

125g small plum cherry tomatoes, such as Datterini

2 tbsp pumpkin seeds

4 tbsp pomegranate seeds

1 small bunch of mint, leaves roughly chopped

1 small bunch of dill, roughly chopped

1 small bunch of flat-leaf parsley, roughly chopped

Finely grated zest and juice of ½ unwaxed lemon

1 tbsp pomegranate molasses

3 tbsp extra virgin olive oil

100g vegan feta (optional), to serve

Cook the freekeh in a pan of boiling salted water for about 25 minutes or until tender. Drain, cool under cold running water, then leave to drain.

Cook the quinoa in another pan of boiling salted water for about 20 minutes or until tender. Drain, cool under cold running water then leave to drain while you prepare the other ingredients.

Heat 1 tbsp of the olive oil in a wok or large frying pan over a medium–high heat. Add half the aubergine and cook, stirring frequently, until soft and golden brown all over. Repeat with the remaining aubergine and olive oil. Tip into a large bowl. Add the cherry tomatoes to the hot pan and cook for a minute or two until starting to soften and the skins are nicely charred. Add to the aubergines with the well-drained freekeh and quinoa.

Toast the pumpkin seeds in the wok over a medium heat for about 30 seconds until they start to pop. Add them to the salad along with the pomegranate seeds, chopped herbs and lemon zest. Mix to combine.

In a small bowl lightly whisk together the lemon juice, pomegranate molasses and extra virgin olive oil. Season well with salt and freshly ground black pepper and pour over the salad. Mix well to combine and leave the salad to sit for 30 minutes for the ingredients to absorb all the flavours. Serve topped with crumbled vegan feta, if you like.

KALE AND LENTIL SALAD
WITH DATES AND GREEN OLIVES

This salad improves over time so make it in the morning if you plan to serve it for lunch to allow all the flavours to mingle. Raisins would work here in place of the dates and you could add the finely chopped skin of a preserved lemon for some extra tang.

SERVES 4–6

100g pecan nuts

2 fat garlic cloves, sliced

3 pared strips unwaxed
   lemon zest and juice of
   ½ lemon

1 tsp cumin seeds

1 tsp coriander seeds

4 tbsp extra virgin olive oil

175g Puy lentils, rinsed
   in cold running water
   and drained

150g leafy kale, washed
   and dried, tough central
   stems removed

5 Medjool or other soft
   dates, pitted and chopped

120g pitted green olives,
   chopped

4 guindilla chillies from a
   jar, drained and chopped

2–3 tbsp roughly chopped
   coriander, plus extra
   to garnish

1 ripe avocado, halved,
   stoned and peeled, to serve

Salt and freshly ground
   black pepper

Toast the pecans in a small frying pan over a medium heat, stirring frequently, for about 2 minutes until they are starting to brown and crisp. Tip the nuts onto a board and roughly chop.

Tip the garlic, lemon zest, cumin and coriander seeds into the frying pan, add the olive oil and warm over a low heat for 1 minute. Remove the pan from the heat and leave the oil to infuse for at least 30 minutes while you prepare the remaining ingredients.

Cook the lentils in boiling salted water for about 25 minutes or according to the packet instructions until just tender.

Meanwhile, tear or slice the kale leaves into bite-size pieces, tip into a large bowl and massage with your hands for 30 seconds – this softens the leaves and breaks down the tough fibres. Add the dates, olives and chillies to the bowl.

Drain the lentils through a sieve and rinse under cold running water to stop them overcooking. Leave to drain thoroughly.

Strain the garlicky spiced oil into a small bowl, pressing down on the lemon zest and garlic to extract as much flavour as possible. Add the lemon juice to the oil, season well with salt and freshly ground black pepper and whisk to combine.

Tip the lentils into the bowl with the kale, pour over the dressing, add the chopped coriander and pecans and mix to combine. Cover and leave the salad for at least 30 minutes before serving.

Spoon the salad onto serving plates and top with sliced avocado and fresh coriander leaves.

ROAST ACORN SQUASH AND PURPLE SPROUTING BROCCOLI
WITH HAZELNUT AND TAHINI DRESSING

This flavour-packed dish makes a wonderful winter salad served warm or at room temperature. Be sure to have plenty of chargrilled sourdough bread alongside to mop up the dressing. This dressing is also delicious spooned over roasted cauliflower florets, romanesco, roasted sprouts or charred hispi (pointed) cabbage.

SERVES 6

1 acorn or small kabocha
   squash
2–3 tbsp olive oil
1 bushy sprig of thyme,
   leaves picked
200g purple sprouting
   broccoli, trimmed
40g currants

DRESSING

50g blanched hazelnuts or
   walnuts
2 garlic cloves
3 tbsp extra virgin olive oil
2 tbsp tahini
1 tbsp non-pareille
   capers, drained
1 tbsp sherry or red
   wine vinegar
1 tsp date or dark
   agave syrup
Salt and freshly ground
   black pepper

Preheat the oven to 170°C fan/190°C/gas mark 5 and line a large baking tray with foil.

Halve the squash, scoop out the seeds and fibres and cut into 2cm-thick wedges or slices. Tip onto the lined baking tray, drizzle with 2 tbsp olive oil, scatter with thyme leaves, season and toss to coat the pieces in oil. Arrange in a single layer on the tray and roast for about 30 minutes until tender and starting to turn golden brown at the edges.

Add the purple sprouting broccoli to the baking tray, lightly drizzle with a little more oil and roast for 5 minutes until starting to char and wilt. Add the currants to the tray and cook for a further 3 minutes to warm and plump the fruit.

Meanwhile, make the dressing. Toast the nuts in a small roasting tin for 4–5 minutes until golden, roughly chop while still warm and tip into a bowl. Finely grate the garlic over the hot nuts, add the extra virgin oil and tahini and mix to coat. Set aside to cool slightly.

Roughly chop the capers, add to the nuts with the vinegar and date syrup, season well and mix to combine.

Arrange the roasted vegetables on a serving plate or individual plates, spoon over the dressing and serve.

RUNNER BEAN SALAD

The season for runner beans is short, so do make the most of them while you can. In this pretty salad they are combined with radishes — another gem of the early summer veggie garden.

SERVES 4

300g runner beans,
   trimmed and cut on
   the diagonal into
   5mm-thick slices
50g whole almonds
1 small fennel bulb,
   trimmed and finely sliced
2 small shallots, finely sliced
6 radishes, finely sliced
1 unwaxed lemon
1 garlic clove, crushed
2 tsp wholegrain mustard
4 tbsp extra virgin olive oil
4 bushy sprigs of mint,
   leaves shredded
Salt and freshly ground
   black pepper

Bring a pan of salted water to the boil, add the beans and cook for 1–2 minutes until al dente. Drain and refresh under running cold water.

Leave the beans to dry on kitchen paper while you prepare the remaining ingredients.

Toast the almonds in a dry frying pan over a medium heat for 2–3 minutes, stirring frequently, until crisp and starting to brown. Remove from the heat and cut into slivers.

Tip the fennel, shallots and radishes into a large bowl, add the runner beans and mix to combine.

Finely grate the zest from the lemon into a small bowl, add 1½ tbsp lemon juice, the crushed garlic and mustard and mix to combine. Add the extra virgin olive oil, season well with salt and freshly ground black pepper and whisk to combine. Pour the dressing over the vegetables, add the chopped almonds and shredded mint and mix to combine. Arrange on a serving dish and enjoy!

CAESAR SALAD
WITH CHARRED SPRING ONIONS, AVOCADO AND CAPERS

Caesar salad is a perennial favourite and the original recipe uses anchovies, eggs and Parmesan in the creamy dressing. In this vegan version you'll not notice their absence. Silken tofu makes a wonderful creamy dressing while mustard, nutritional yeast and tahini (or miso) bring a big savoury flavour and crispy capers add a hit of saltiness.

SERVES 4—6

4 Little Gem lettuces
1 bunch of spring
   onions, trimmed
2—3 tbsp olive oil
½ ciabatta loaf, thinly sliced
1 tbsp capers, drained
   and patted dry on
   kitchen paper
1 ripe avocado, halved,
   stoned and peeled
½ cucumber

DRESSING

150g silken tofu
2 rounded tsp Dijon
   mustard
Juice of ½ lemon
1 fat garlic clove, crushed
1 tbsp tahini or white miso
2 tsp nutritional yeast, plus
   extra to serve
3 tbsp fruity olive oil
Salt and freshly ground
   black pepper

Separate the lettuce leaves, wash in cold water, drain, cover and chill until ready to use.

Brush the spring onions with 1 tbsp of the olive oil. Heat a ridged griddle pan over a medium—high heat, add the spring onions and cook, turning once or twice, for about 3 minutes until softened and nicely charred. Remove from the pan. Brush the ciabatta slices with 1 tbsp olive oil and toast on both sides in the hot griddle pan to make large croûtons.

Heat a little olive oil in a small frying pan over a medium—high heat, add the capers and cook for a minute or so until golden and crisp. Drain on kitchen paper.

To make the dressing put all the ingredients into a food processor and blend until smooth. Add 1—2 tsp water if the dressing is very thick — it should be coating consistency.

Cut the avocado and cucumber into bite-size pieces. Spoon most of the dressing over the salad leaves and toss to coat. Pile the leaves, avocado and cucumber onto plates and top with the charred spring onions, croûtons and crispy capers. Scatter with a little nutritional yeast and serve the remaining dressing alongside.

BRUSSELS SPROUT, RED CABBAGE AND CHICORY SLAW

This is a wintry slaw that wouldn't be out of place at a festive buffet and makes good use of Brussels sprouts, which essentially are mini cabbages. The nuts are interchangeable — you could just as well use walnuts or pecans if that's what you have to hand; equally the pear could be swapped for a crisp eating apple.

SERVES 6—8

200g Brussels sprouts, trimmed
¼ small red cabbage, trimmed and tough core removed
2 red chicory
1 crisp pear, cored and sliced into thick matchsticks
Seeds from ½ pomegranate
75g blanched hazelnuts, toasted and roughly chopped
2 tbsp roughly chopped flat-leaf parsley
1 tbsp roughly chopped tarragon leaves
4 tbsp hazelnut or walnut oil
Juice of ½ lemon
2 tsp wholegrain mustard
1 tsp pomegranate molasses
Salt and freshly ground black pepper

Finely shred the sprouts and red cabbage and combine in a large mixing bowl. Separate the leaves of the chicory and add to the bowl, along with the pear, most of the pomegranate seeds (save some for garnish), the hazelnuts and three-quarters of the herbs. Mix gently to combine.

In a small bowl whisk together the oil, lemon juice, mustard and pomegranate molasses. Season well with salt and freshly ground black pepper and pour over the salad. Mix to combine and leave for 3—4 minutes before spooning onto a serving plate. Top with the reserved pomegranate seeds and herbs to serve.

BEANS, SUGAR SNAPS AND PEAS
WITH LIME, MISO AND GARLIC DRESSING

This salad is garnished with crispy fried garlic, which packs a punch — if you prefer your garlic more subtle, simply add half a crushed clove to the dressing instead. Add the dressing to the salad just before serving, to retain the vibrant green colour of the peas and beans.

SERVES 6

200g fine green
  beans, trimmed
200g sugar snaps
150g fresh peas (podded
  weight) or frozen
4 tbsp sunflower oil
2 garlic cloves, finely sliced
2 spring onions, trimmed,
  halved and finely shredded
Finely grated zest and juice
  of 1 unwaxed lime
1 tbsp white miso
2–3 tsp grated fresh ginger
3 tbsp avocado oil
1 tsp tamari
1 avocado, halved, stoned
  and peeled
2 tsp toasted sesame seeds,
  to serve

Bring a saucepan of salted water to the boil. Add the fine beans and cook for 1 minute. Add the sugar snaps and cook for a further minute, then remove from the pan with a slotted spoon and plunge into a bowl of iced water to stop them cooking further. Once the veggies are completely cold drain well.

Cook the peas in the boiling water for about 2 minutes until tender — if using frozen peas they will take half the time. Drain and refresh under cold running water.

Cut the beans and sugar snaps in half on the diagonal and tip into a bowl with the drained peas.

Heat the sunflower oil in a frying pan over a medium heat. Add the garlic and fry, stirring constantly, until crisp and golden. Remove from the pan with a slotted spoon and drain on kitchen paper. Add the shredded spring onion and cook until golden. Drain and set aside.

In a small bowl combine the lime zest and juice, miso, ginger, avocado oil and tamari. Cut the avocado into bite-size pieces and add to the peas and beans. Pour over the dressing and mix gently to combine.

Arrange on a serving dish and scatter with the crispy garlic, spring onions and toasted sesame seeds.

VIETNAMESE RICE NOODLE SALAD

SERVES 4

100g rice vermicelli noodles

3 tbsp rice vinegar

Juice of 1 lime

3 tbsp soy sauce

3 tsp agave syrup or soft light brown sugar

2 tsp vegan fish sauce (optional)

3 tsp grated fresh ginger

1 bird's eye chilli, deseeded or left seeded, finely sliced

1 garlic clove, crushed

½ cucumber, halved lengthways, seeds scooped out and discarded

2 carrots

1 Little Gem lettuce, cut into fine strips

100g sugar snaps, trimmed and halved on the diagonal

3 spring onions, trimmed and finely sliced

6 radishes, trimmed and finely sliced

8 cherry tomatoes, halved

100g beansprouts, rinsed

1 mild red chilli (optional), deseeded and finely sliced

3 tbsp mint leaves

3 tbsp coriander leaves

3 tbsp Thai basil leaves

50g roasted peanuts, roughly chopped

This crisp, refreshing salad is very pretty. An authentic Vietnamese salad would include fish sauce in the dressing, so vegan fish sauce is an optional inclusion; it's not entirely necessary but it does give an added layer of flavour. If your tolerance and preference for chillies is high then leave the seeds in the bird's eye chilli. The easiest, neatest and quickest way to julienne vegetables is by using a special vegetable peeler with a julienne blade — these are inexpensive and easily available in large cookware stores or online.

Put the noodles into a heatproof bowl, cover with freshly boiled water and set aside to soften for 10 minutes. Drain and refresh under running cold water. Leave to drain in a colander while you prepare the other ingredients.

To make the dressing combine the rice vinegar, lime juice, soy sauce, agave syrup, fish sauce (if using), ginger, chilli and garlic in a bowl.

Cut the cucumber and carrots into julienned strips. Combine with the other prepared vegetables and chilli (if using) in a bowl and add the herbs.

Divide the noodles between individual bowls or arrange on one sharing plate. Top with the veggies and herbs, spoon over two-thirds of the dressing, scatter with peanuts and serve with extra dressing on the side.

ROAST BEETROOT AND GRAPE SALAD

The nutty crumble in this salad makes more than you will need, but it's incredibly moreish and would be rather nice to serve with drinks. Grapes become extra sweet and juicy when roasted, and are a wonderful contrast to the earthy beetroot, spicy crumble and salty cheese. This will keep well in an airtight container for a week. Add some fresh figs and wild rocket or other bitter, peppery leaves to the salad if you like, and if your beetroot has delicate, crisp leaves, add those, too.

SERVES 6

50g pecan nuts
50g almonds
50g pistachios
40g pumpkin seeds
20g golden linseeds
20g sunflower seeds
20g sesame seeds
10g poppy seeds
2 tbsp maple syrup
1 tbsp sunflower or olive oil
1 tsp cumin seeds
½ tsp smoked paprika
1 bunch beetroot (about
    5 small–medium), ideally
    with leaves
1 small bunch (350g) black
    seedless grapes
3 tbsp extra virgin olive oil
1 tbsp balsamic vinegar
3 red chicory
100g vegan Greek-style
    cheese, crumbled
Sea salt flakes and freshly
    ground black pepper

Preheat the oven to 160°C fan/180°C/gas mark 4 and line a baking tray with baking paper.

Start by making the nutty crumble. Roughly chop all the nuts, tip into a bowl and add the seeds, maple syrup, oil, cumin seeds and paprika. Season well with sea salt flakes and freshly ground black pepper and mix well. Spread out on the lined baking tray and roast in the oven for about 20 minutes, stirring halfway through until the mixture is crisp and is starting to caramelize and clump together. Leave to cool and then store either in a jar or airtight container until ready to serve.

Trim any leaves and stalks off the beetroot, washing and chilling any nice small leaves for the salad. Place the whole beetroots in a small, foil-lined roasting tin, season and add a splash of water. Cover and roast for about 40 minutes until tender when tested with the point of a knife. Leave to cool and then carefully remove the skins – they should rub off easily between your hands. Cut each beetroot into bite-size wedges.

Separate the grapes into smaller bunches of 3 or 4 grapes and place in another foil-lined roasting tin. Drizzle with 3 tbsp extra virgin olive oil, season and roast for about 30 minutes until soft and juicy. Lift the grapes from the pan, leaving the roasting juices behind. Whisk the balsamic into the pan juices and leave the grapes and dressing to cool to room temperature.

Separate the chicory leaves and arrange on plates with any reserved beetroot leaves. Settle the beetroot wedges and roasted grapes among the leaves and scatter over the cheese. Drizzle with dressing and scatter with nutty crumble to serve.

SHAVED BROCCOLI SALAD
WITH SEED-COATED AVOCADO

This is a super green salad with a zippy dressing. Look out for firm, crisp broccoli as you will be using both the stalk and frilly top in this no-waste salad. The broccoli is served with avocado halves that are coated in crisp, toasted sesame seeds but if you prefer you could also use Furikake if you have some (see page 160). I love soft lettuce, which is much underused these days, and it is cheaper and less wasteful than buying prepacked salad leaves.

SERVES 4

1 head of broccoli
   (about 300g)
1 small bunch of coriander,
   chopped, reserving a few
   leaves for garnish
Finely grated zest and juice
   of 1 unwaxed lime
3 spring onions, trimmed
   and finely sliced
1 mild green chilli, deseeded
   and finely sliced
30g flaked almonds, toasted
1 garlic clove, finely grated
3cm piece fresh ginger,
   finely grated
4 tbsp avocado oil
1½ tsp agave syrup
2 avocados
1 tbsp toasted sesame seeds
1 tbsp toasted black
   sesame seeds
1 soft-leaf lettuce, leaves
   separated, washed
   and chilled
Salt and freshly ground
   black pepper

Cut the broccoli stalks from the florets then, using a very sharp knife or vegetable peeler, cut all of the stalk lengthways into wafer-thin slices. Tip into a large bowl. Cut the florets into thin slices and add to the bowl, along with the coriander, lime zest, spring onions, chilli and flaked almonds. Mix to combine.

Pour the lime juice into a small bowl, reserving 2 tsp. Add the garlic and ginger to the bowl, then the avocado oil and agave syrup, season well with salt and freshly ground black pepper and mix with a fork. Spoon three-quarters of the dressing over the broccoli and mix well. Cover and chill for 30 minutes to allow the flavours to mingle.

Halve, stone and peel the avocados. Combine the sesame seeds in a shallow bowl. Brush the outside of each avocado half with the reserved lime juice and press into the seeds to coat.

Arrange the lettuce leaves in four salad bowls and spoon the broccoli salad to one side. Place one avocado half in each bowl, cut-side uppermost, and spoon a little of the reserved dressing into the hole to serve.

POTATO SALAD WITH PRESERVED LEMON
GREEN CHILLI, PISTACHIO AND HARISSA DRESSING

I've never been a fan of cold potato salad dressed with mayonnaise — but I can eat a bowl of cold roast potatoes quite happily! Add a punchy, spicy dressing and handfuls of fresh herbs to still-warm, roasted and squashed potatoes and you're suddenly in a whole new world of potato salad appreciation.

SERVES 4

700g new potatoes
1–2 tbsp olive oil
2 tsp za'atar
2 small or 1 large
   preserved lemon
1 mild green chilli, deseeded
   and finely chopped
50g unsalted pistachio nuts,
   roughly chopped
1 tbsp capers
5 spring onions, trimmed
   and thinly sliced
1 tbsp harissa
1 garlic clove, crushed
3 tbsp extra virgin olive oil
Juice of ½ lemon
1 small bunch of mint,
   leaves picked
1 small bunch coriander
A good handful – about 50g –
   watercress
Salt and freshly ground
   black pepper

Preheat the oven to 170°C fan/190°C/gas mark 5.

Put the whole potatoes into a roasting tin, drizzle with olive oil, scatter with za'atar and season with salt and freshly ground black pepper. Roast for about 40 minutes, shaking the pan from time to time, until the skins are golden brown and crisp and the potatoes are tender. Leave to cool slightly and then lightly squash the potatoes using a fish slice. Tip into a large bowl.

Meanwhile, cut the preserved lemons in half, scoop out and discard the soft middle and any seeds and finely shred the skin. Add to the bowl, along with the chilli, pistachios, capers and spring onions.

In a small bowl use a fork to whisk together the harissa, garlic, extra virgin olive oil and lemon juice. Season with salt and freshly ground black pepper. Pour the dressing over the potato mixture and stir gently to combine. Leave for 10 minutes for all the flavours to be absorbed.

Scatter with the mint, coriander and watercress, mix gently and serve.

CUCUMBER SALAD

Serve this simple, utterly delicious salad with a pile of warm toasted pitta bread and perhaps some dressed tomatoes alongside. You will be transported to a Greek taverna, sitting in the sunshine on a golden beach….

SERVES 4

250g dairy-free yogurt
1 small red onion
1 large cucumber, halved
   lengthways then cut into
   4mm-thick slices
3 tbsp roughly chopped dill
2 tbsp roughly chopped mint
Juice of ½ lemon
3 tbsp extra virgin olive oil
½ tsp ground sumac
½ tsp nigella seeds
1 garlic clove, crushed
1 small handful of fennel or
   chive flowers, to garnish
Salt and freshly ground
   black pepper

Line a sieve with a square of clean muslin or an unused J-cloth and set over a bowl. Tip in the yogurt and allow excess liquid to drain into the bowl. Chill for 1–2 hours until the yogurt is slightly firmer – don't leave it any longer, though, or it might become too set.

Meanwhile, slice the red onion into half-moons, tip into a bowl, cover with freshly boiled water and set aside for 5 minutes to lessen the strong flavour. Drain and pat dry on kitchen paper.

Combine the cucumber with the onion slices in a large bowl. Stir in the dill, mint, lemon juice, 2 tbsp olive oil, sumac and nigella seeds. Season with salt and freshly ground black pepper.

Season the strained yogurt, mix in the crushed garlic and spoon onto a serving dish. Pile the cucumber mixture on top, drizzle with the remaining tablespoon of olive oil, scatter with fennel or chive flowers and serve.

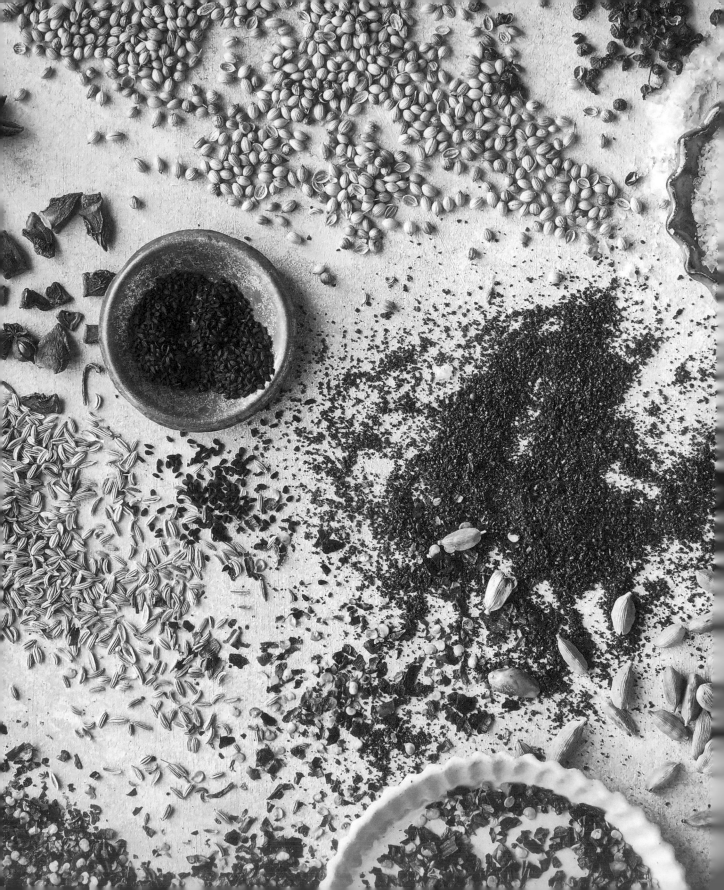

SIDES & SEASONINGS

SHOESTRING POTATOES WITH CHAAT MASALA

It's a challenge not to eat these ultra-skinny crispy potato chips the minute they're out of the pan. They are delicious simply seasoned with sea salt flakes, freshly ground black pepper and perhaps a little finely chopped fresh rosemary, but they take on a higher level of deliciousness when seasoned with chaat masala. You'll make more seasoning mix than you need for this recipe, but it's not worth making in tiny quantities and there are many other uses for it: scatter over lentils, rice or roasted veggies… even over a fresh fruit salad of mango and watermelon.

SERVES 4

500g (3 medium) floury
  potatoes such as Maris
  Piper, scrubbed
1 litre sunflower oil, for
  deep-frying

CHAAT MASALA
1 heaped tsp black
  peppercorns
1 tbsp cumin seeds
½ tbsp coriander seeds
1 tsp fennel seeds
½ tbsp crushed dried
  chilli flakes
1 tbsp amchoor
1 tbsp sea salt flakes
1 tsp garlic granules
¼ tsp asafoetida

Start by making the chaat masala. Tip the peppercorns, cumin, coriander, and fennel seeds in a dry frying pan and toast over a medium heat, stirring constantly, for about 1 minute until toasted and aromatic. Add the chilli flakes and toast for a further 30 seconds.

Use a pestle and mortar to crush the spices. Transfer to a spice grinder or mini food processor and add the remaining ingredients. Pulse until ground into a coarse powder. Store in a lidded jar until ready to use.

Use a mandolin (watch your fingers) to cut the potatoes into matchsticks. Alternatively, julienne finely using a sharp knife. Tip the potatoes into a sieve and rinse well under cold running water. Drain then leave to dry on a double thickness of kitchen paper for about 30 minutes.

Heat the oil to 180°C, either in a deep-fryer or large saucepan. Line a large baking tray or roasting tin with a double or triple thickness of kitchen paper.

Carefully add a handful of chips to the hot oil and fry for about 2 minutes, stirring with a slotted spoon, until crisp and golden. (Don't add too many chips to the hot oil at once, otherwise the temperature will quickly drop and the chips will be soggy rather than crisp.)

Remove the chips from the pan with a slotted spoon and drain on the kitchen paper for 30 seconds, then season with a generous scattering of chaat masala.

Continue to fry the chips in small batches, allowing the oil to come back up to temperature between each addition. Serve the chips as soon after frying as possible.

MSABAHA

Msabaha, pronounced 'musabaha', is usually served for breakfast in the Levant. It is similar to hummus but heavier on the tahini and has whole chickpeas stirred through. My version, which is not entirely authentic, should be served with raw veggies and warmed or chargrilled flatbreads for dipping and scooping. Do remember to soak the chickpeas overnight.

SERVES 4

100g dried chickpeas, soaked overnight in a large bowl of cold water
½ tsp bicarbonate of soda
1 large garlic clove, peeled and roughly chopped
3 tbsp tahini
Juice of ½–1 lemon
1 tsp ground cumin
4–5 tbsp extra virgin olive oil
2 tbsp ice-cold water
½ tsp cayenne pepper
1 tbsp pumpkin seeds
1 tbsp pine kernels
Salt and freshly ground black pepper

TO SERVE

2 small cucumbers, cut into wedges
4 tomatoes, quartered
1 Little Gem lettuce, leaves separated
Quick Flatbreads (see page 158) or pitta, warmed or chargrilled

Drain and rinse the soaked chickpeas, tip into a medium saucepan, add the bicarbonate of soda and cover with fresh water. Bring to the boil, reduce to a simmer and cook for about 40 minutes or until really tender. Remove from the heat and leave to cool in the water before draining.

Spoon 75g of the chickpeas into a bowl, cover and set aside. Tip the rest into a food processor and blend until nearly smooth, scraping down the sides of the bowl from time to time. Add the garlic, tahini, juice of ½ lemon and ½ tsp cumin and whizz again until smooth.

With the mixer still running add 2 tbsp olive oil and 2 tbsp ice-cold water and blend until the mixture is silky smooth, adding a little more oil or water to loosen the mixture if needed. Season with salt and freshly ground black pepper and add more lemon juice to taste.

Spoon the mixture into a serving dish and make swirls in the top using the back of the spoon. Heat 1 tbsp of the remaining olive oil in a small frying pan over a medium heat. Add the reserved chickpeas and fry, stirring frequently until crisp. Add ½ tsp ground cumin, the cayenne, pumpkin seeds and pine kernels and season with salt and freshly ground black pepper. Continue frying for a further minute until the pumpkin seeds pop and the pine kernels and chickpeas are golden. Spoon on top of the msabaha, drizzle with more olive oil and serve while the topping is still warm with cucumber, tomatoes, leaves and flatbreads.

CRISP-FRIED OKRA

These crispy spicy morsels are enough to convince even the most ardent okra-haters that they might be wrong about this curious green veg. Okra has a bad reputation for sliminess but often that just means it's been badly cooked. Here, spiced gram and rice flour give these snacks a deliciously crisp coating – not a bit of slime – making them perfect to serve with a glass of something chilled. Look out for small okra, about the size of your finger; they are often called lady's fingers – so apt.

SERVES 4

200g okra
2 tbsp gram flour
2 tbsp ground rice flour
1 tsp ground turmeric
½ tsp chilli powder
1 tsp cumin seeds
1 tsp nigella seeds
½ tsp garlic granules
Salt and freshly ground
  black pepper
500ml sunflower oil,
  for frying

Rinse the okra in cold water and leave to dry on a double thickness of kitchen paper or a clean tea towel.

In a large bowl combine both flours, the spices, seeds and garlic and a good grinding of black pepper – do not add salt at this stage.

Top and tail the okra and cut each one in half from top to toe. Tip into the spice mixture and use your hands to mix so that each piece of okra is coated in spiced flour. Set aside for 10 minutes.

Heat the oil in a wok or large saucepan until a piece of okra sizzles on contact with the oil.

Drizzle 1 tbsp water over the okra and lightly mix with your hands so that the coating becomes very slightly damp and clumpy and sticks to the okra. Carefully drop a small batch of the okra in the hot oil and cook, turning frequently with a slotted spoon, for about 2 minutes or until golden brown and crisp. Lift the okra from the oil with the slotted spoon, drain on kitchen paper and season with salt. Continue cooking the rest in small batches, allowing the oil to reheat after each batch.

Serve as soon after cooking as possible.

FENNEL BRAISED
WITH TOMATOES

A large ovenproof sauté pan is ideal for cooking this dish — failing that, fry the fennel then transfer to a large gratin dish that will hold the fennel snugly in a single layer.

SERVES 4—6

2 fennel bulbs, trimmed,
  leafy fronds reserved
2—3 tbsp olive oil
1 onion, sliced
1 large garlic clove, sliced
200ml vegetable stock
100ml white wine
1 sprig of thyme
2 bay leaves
12 cherry tomatoes
1 red pepper, deseeded
  and sliced
2 heaped tsp small capers
2 tbsp roughly chopped
  flat-leaf parsley
Salt and freshly ground
  black pepper

Preheat the oven to 160°C fan/180°C/gas mark 4.

Cut the fennel bulbs in half from root to tip and then into slices 1—2cm thick.

Heat 1 tbsp of the olive oil in a large ovenproof sauté pan over a medium heat. Add the fennel slices and fry on both sides until golden. Depending on the size of your pan, you may need to do this in batches, adding more oil as needed. Remove the fennel from the pan. Add another tablespoon of oil, the onion and garlic and cook for about 5 minutes until tender and starting to brown at the edges.

Return the fennel to the pan. Pour the stock and wine around the veggies, season well, add the thyme and bay leaves and bring to the boil. Cover with foil and cook in the oven for 30 minutes until starting to soften.

Remove the foil, add the whole cherry tomatoes, pepper and capers. Cook for a further 20—25 minutes until the fennel is tender and the tomatoes are starting to burst.

Scatter with parsley and any reserved fennel fronds and serve.

BRAISED LITTLE GEM LETTUCE WITH PEAS, BEANS AND MINT

This wonderful side dish can also make an early summer lunch. If you are using fresh peas, don't throw away the pods, as they make a wonderful light stock. Young broad beans are best for this so if yours are on the large side, remove the outer grey skins to reveal the tender green beans within.

SERVES 4—6

100g dried flageolet beans,
  soaked in a large bowl of
  cold water overnight, or
  1 x 400g can, drained
  and rinsed
1 tbsp olive oil
3 spring onions, trimmed
  and cut into 1cm slices
1 garlic clove, crushed
150g peas
100g young broad beans
  (podded weight)
300ml vegetable stock
Juice of ½ lemon
3 Little Gem lettuces, halved
1—2 tbsp roughly chopped
  mint leaves
1 tbsp extra virgin olive oil
Salt and freshly ground
  black pepper

If using dried flageolet beans, drain and rinse the soaked beans, put in a pan over a medium heat, cover with fresh water and simmer for about 40 minutes or until tender, then drain.

Heat the olive oil in a large saucepan, add the spring onions and garlic and cook over a low—medium heat for about 3 minutes until tender but not coloured. Add the peas, broad beans, flageolet beans, vegetable stock and lemon juice. Season with salt and freshly ground black pepper, mix to combine and heat to a gentle simmer. Add the lettuce halves, cover the pan with a disc of baking paper and cook for about 10 minutes until the lettuce is tender when tested with the point of a knife.

Scatter with fresh mint and drizzle with extra virgin olive oil to serve.

MAMA GANOUSH

Baba ganoush's sibling… in this case it's courgettes, not aubergines, cooked until softened and the skin is charred then the whole lot is blended with tahini and garlic. I have given a method for cooking the courgettes under a conventional grill but feel free to cook them over a barbecue or on a ridged griddle pan if you have it heated for other things. Serve mama ganoush scattered with fresh mint leaves and toasted pine kernels and perhaps a handful of pomegranate seeds for colour.

SERVES 4–6

2 large courgettes, trimmed

4 tbsp extra virgin olive oil, plus extra to serve

1 garlic clove, crushed

Juice of ½ lemon

1 tbsp tahini paste

2 tbsp chopped mint leaves, plus extra whole leaves to serve

2 tbsp chopped flat-leaf parsley

25g pine kernels, toasted, to serve

Salt and freshly ground black pepper

Preheat the grill to high. Halve the courgettes lengthways and place on a foil-lined tray. Brush with 1 tbsp extra virgin olive oil and cook under the hot grill for about 4 minutes on each side until soft, brown all over and just starting to char in places.

Leave the courgettes to cool slightly and then tip into a food processor with the remaining olive oil, the garlic, lemon juice, tahini and chopped herbs. Season well with salt and freshly ground black pepper and whizz until nearly smooth.

Taste and add more seasoning or lemon juice as needed then spoon the mama ganoush into a serving bowl and leave to cool to room temperature.

Scatter with toasted pine kernels and mint leaves and drizzle with extra virgin olive oil to serve.

TOMATO KASUNDI

This Indian spiced tomato relish is delicious served with just about anything savoury — but is wonderful with burgers, in sandwiches or alongside the Butternut Squash Nut Roast (see page 62), the Tenderstem, Kale and Courgette Pakora (see page 108) or even spooned onto dahl.

MAKES 2 JARS

2 tsp cumin seeds
1 tsp coriander seeds
3 tbsp sunflower oil
1 tbsp black mustard seeds
1 tsp ground turmeric
A good pinch of crushed
 dried chilli flakes
5cm piece fresh
 ginger, grated
4 garlic cloves, crushed
1 red chilli, finely chopped,
 with or without the seeds
1 green chilli, finely
 chopped, with or
 without the seeds
1 large onion, finely
 chopped
2 crisp eating apples, peeled,
 cored and finely chopped
1kg ripe tomatoes, cored
 and diced
200ml cider vinegar
125g soft brown sugar
1 tsp salt
Freshly ground black pepper

Toast the cumin and coriander seeds in a dry pan until they start to smell aromatic and then grind using a pestle and mortar.

Heat the oil in a large saucepan, add the cumin, coriander and mustard seeds, turmeric and chilli flakes and cook for 30 seconds over a medium heat. Add the ginger, garlic and chillies, cook, stirring constantly, for a minute and then add the onion. Cook for a further 5 minutes to soften.

Add the apples and tomatoes to the pan with the vinegar, sugar, salt and season with a generous grinding of black pepper. Bring to the boil, reduce the heat to a simmer and continue to cook for 40 minutes, stirring often, or until the apples, onions and tomatoes have broken down and cooked to a chutney and only a small amount of liquid remains.

Spoon into sterilized jars, seal and store in the fridge until needed. Once opened your kasundi should be kept in the fridge and eaten within a month.

Note: The easiest way to sterilize jars is to put them in the dishwasher on the hottest setting and leave them to dry. Alternatively, you can put them in a pan of boiling water for a few minutes (leave to dry on a clean tea towel) or wash the jars in hot soapy water, drain and place on a tray in a low oven for 10 minutes.

POLENTA WITH ROASTED CORN

In this recipe sweetcorn has a dual role — the chargrilled kernels are stirred through creamy polenta and the cobs used to make a delicious stock in which the polenta is cooked. Summer is corn on the cob season so if you happen to have the barbecue lit it's worth cooking the corn at the same time and saving it for later. Try to buy corn on the cob still in its leafy green husks — that's a sign of freshness and the kernels should be plump, juicy and full of flavour. Soft polenta is often served with grated Parmesan stirred through just before serving — try adding grated vegan Italian-style cheese or a spoonful of vegan cream cheese.

SERVES 4—6

2 large corn on the cob,
    husks removed, trimmed
2 tbsp olive oil
1 bay leaf
4 black peppercorns
3 spring onions, trimmed
    and cut into 1cm slices
2 garlic cloves, thinly sliced
½ tsp smoked paprika
175g instant or quick-cook
    polenta
2 tsp nutritional yeast
Salt and freshly ground
    black pepper

Preheat a ridged griddle pan over a medium heat. Lightly brush the corn cobs with 1 tbsp of the olive oil and cook on the hot griddle pan, turning frequently, for about 10 minutes until the kernels are tender and nicely charred. Remove from the pan and leave to cool.

Once the sweetcorn is cool enough to handle stand the cobs upright on a chopping board and use a sharp knife to shave the kernels from the cob. Scoop the kernels into a bowl and set aside.

Place the shaved corn cobs in a large saucepan, cover with 800ml water, add the bay leaf and black peppercorns and bring to the boil over a medium heat. Reduce the heat to a low simmer and cook the stock for 30 minutes to an hour to extract as much flavour as possible from the cobs.

Heat the remaining 1 tbsp olive oil in a large saucepan over a low—medium heat. Add the spring onions and garlic and cook, stirring often, for about 3 minutes until the onions and garlic are golden. Stir in the smoked paprika, cook for 30 seconds, and then remove from the pan and add to the reserved corn kernels.

Strain the corn stock into the pan and bring to the boil. Slowly and steadily pour the polenta into the hot stock, whisking constantly, until smooth and thoroughly combined. Reduce the heat to low and continue cooking, whisking for 5 minutes until the polenta is smooth and the consistency of soft mashed potato, adding a little more water if needed. Add the reserved corn, spring onions and garlic, season with the nutritional yeast, salt and freshly ground black pepper and mix to combine. Continue to cook for a further 2 minutes, taste and add more seasoning as needed — polenta needs more seasoning than you think.

QUICK 'KIMCHI'

Kimchi is a Korean side dish of fermented vegetables, usually Chinese leaf, and is seasoned with chilli flakes, garlic and ginger. Traditionally the cabbage is softened in brine, rinsed and then mixed with a chilli, garlic and ginger paste often thickened with rice flour. This recipe is inspired by kimchi and uses similar seasoning but requires less brining and fermenting and can be eaten the day after making. It will keep, sealed, for up to two weeks in the fridge.

MAKES ABOUT 20 SERVINGS

1 Chinese leaf cabbage, trimmed and cut into large bite-size pieces

2 tbsp salt

1 carrot, peeled and sliced into thick matchsticks

1 tennis-ball size kohlrabi, peeled and sliced into thick matchsticks

4 spring onions, trimmed and thinly sliced

3 garlic cloves, roughly chopped

4cm piece ginger, peeled and roughly chopped

2 tbsp vegan fish sauce

1 tbsp rice vinegar

1 tbsp gochujang paste

1 heaped tbsp Korean chilli flakes (gochugaru)

½ tbsp caster sugar

2 tsp soy sauce or tamari

Tip the Chinese leaf into a large bowl, add the salt and mix to combine. Boil the kettle, leave to cool for 3 minutes then pour hot water over the Chinese leaf to cover. Leave to brine for 30 minutes while you prepare the remaining ingredients.

Combine the prepared carrot, kohlrabi and spring onions in a bowl. Scrape the garlic and ginger into a small food processor. Add the remaining ingredients and blend until smooth.

Drain the Chinese leaf and rinse very well under cold running water. Drain well and add to the carrot mixture. Add the chilli paste mixture and mix well to coat. Scoop into an airtight box and chill for 24 hours before serving.

CHARRED LEEKS AND ASPARAGUS
WITH ROMESCO SAUCE

Romesco sauce is a smoky tomato and red pepper sauce from the Spanish region of Catalonia, where it is often served with grilled fish. It's just as delicious with chargrilled or barbecued vegetables.

SERVES 6

1 bunch asparagus spears, trimmed
6 baby leeks, trimmed
1 bunch salad onions, trimmed
1 tbsp olive oil
Fresh fennel flowers (if available), to garnish

ROMESCO SAUCE

2 large red peppers, deseeded and quartered
5 tbsp extra virgin olive oil
3 garlic cloves
250g ripe tomatoes
½ tsp smoked paprika, plus extra to taste
50g blanched almonds, toasted, plus extra for garnish
25g blanched hazelnuts, toasted, plus extra for garnish
1 tbsp sherry vinegar
1 tbsp roughly chopped flat-leaf parsley
1 tbsp lemon juice, if needed
Salt and freshly ground black pepper

Start by making the sauce. Preheat the grill. Place the peppers on a baking tray, skin-side up. Drizzle with 1 tbsp of the olive oil and cook under the grill until the skins are blackened and blistered. Tip into a bowl, cover with clingfilm and set aside for 10 minutes.

Heat the remaining olive oil in a sauté pan, add the garlic cloves and cook over a low heat for about 5–10 minutes until tender but not coloured. Meanwhile, peel and roughly chop the grilled peppers.

Cut a small cross on the base of each tomato, place in a bowl and cover with boiling water. Leave for 1 minute then drain under cold running water to loosen the skins. Peel and roughly chop the tomatoes, add to the sauté pan with the smoked paprika and cook for a further 5 minutes until softened and most of the tomato juice has been reduced and cooked off.

Tip the contents of the pan into a blender or food processor, add the peppers, nuts, vinegar and parsley and whizz until nearly smooth. Taste, season and add more smoked paprika and a squeeze of lemon juice if needed. Pour into a bowl, cover and chill but bring back to room temperature to serve.

When you're ready to eat, heat a ridged griddle pan over a high heat. Toss the asparagus, leeks and salad onions in the olive oil and cook on the hot griddle pan, turning frequently, until nicely charred all over. Season and arrange on a serving plate. Spoon over some of the romesco sauce, roughly chop the almonds and hazelnuts, scatter over the top, garnish with fennel flowers if available, and serve with extra sauce alongside.

RUNNER BEANS WITH TOMATOES
AND DILL, MINT AND TOASTED ALMONDS

These delicious beans would be perfect as part of a Mediterranean salad spread with the Farinata on page 111, Beetroot and Spinach Falafel on page 101 and Freekeh and Quinoa Tabbouleh on page 117, and served with chargrilled bread for mopping up the tomato sauce. The beans will lose their vibrant green colour during cooking but what they lose in colour they make up for in flavour. If you have a glut of courgettes you could use those in place of the runner beans.

SERVES 4–6

2 banana shallots,
   thinly sliced
2 tbsp fruity olive oil
1 large garlic clove, crushed
A pinch of dried oregano
A pinch of dried mint
100ml dry white wine
200ml vegetable stock
1 x 400g can chopped
   tomatoes
2 pared strips lemon zest
½ tsp sugar
250g runner beans,
   trimmed and cut on the
   diagonal into 2cm slices
Salt and freshly ground
   black pepper

TO SERVE
1 heaped tbsp roughly
   chopped dill
1 heaped tbsp roughly
   chopped mint
50g flaked almonds, toasted

Cook the shallots in 1 tbsp of the olive oil in a large sauté pan over a medium heat for about 5 minutes, stirring frequently, until softened and just starting to brown. Add the crushed garlic, dried oregano and mint and cook for a further minute.

Add the wine, stock, tomatoes, lemon zest and sugar and season well with salt and freshly ground black pepper. Stir to combine and bring to the boil, then simmer for about 10 minutes until reduced slightly. Add the beans to the pan, stir to combine and continue to cook for 8–10 minutes until the beans are tender.

Add salt and pepper as needed and leave to cool until warm or at room temperature. Serve scattered with chopped dill, mint and flaked almonds.

SCORCHED GREEN TOMATO SALSA

If you grow your own tomatoes you will no doubt be happy to find a recipe for using up that glut that refuses to ripen at the end of the summer and doesn't involve making jars and jars of chutney. This fresh salsa is a riff on tomatillo salsa or salsa verde, which is served in Mexico with tortilla chips.

SERVES 4

1 small onion, chopped
500g large green (unripe) tomatoes, halved
1 large green chilli, halved
1 garlic clove, chopped
Juice of ½–1 lime
1 small bunch of coriander, chopped
Salt and freshly ground black pepper

Chop the onion, tip into a bowl, cover with freshly boiled water and leave to soak for 15 minutes.

Preheat the grill to medium–high. Place the tomatoes, cut-side down, on a foil-lined baking tray. Cook under the grill for 4–5 minutes until the skin is charred and the tomatoes are starting to soften.

Turn the tomatoes over, put the chilli halves on the tray, skin-side up, and return to the heat for a further 3 minutes until the tomatoes are softened and juicy and the chilli skin is browned. Leave to cool slightly and then roughly chop both the tomatoes and chilli.

Drain the onion and tip into a food processor along with garlic and pulse until finely chopped. Add the tomatoes, chilli, juice of ½ lime and season well with salt and freshly ground black pepper.

Add the chopped coriander and pulse to combine. Taste and add more seasoning or lime juice as needed. Serve with tortilla chips or fried flour tortillas (see page 95) for dipping.

SRI LANKAN GREEN BEAN CURRY

This is a vibrant, lightly spiced bean curry to serve alongside aromatic coconut rice. This recipe uses a mixture of runner and green beans but feel free to use the full quantity of one type if that is your preference. If you want a milder curry, omit the crushed dried chilli flakes and remove the seeds from the green chilli. Fresh curry leaves are available in larger supermarkets, Indian supermarkets or from specialist online grocers. (It's worth buying extra and keeping them in the freezer in an airtight bag or box.)

SERVES 6

1 tbsp coconut oil

3 shallots, finely sliced

2 garlic cloves, crushed

3 tsp grated ginger

1 green chilli, finely chopped (seeds included or removed)

1 tsp black mustard seeds

1 tsp turmeric

1 tsp ground cumin

½ tsp crushed dried chilli flakes

10 curry leaves

1 x 400ml can of full-fat coconut milk

½–1 tsp coconut or soft light brown sugar

Juice of ½ lime

300g mix of runner and green beans, trimmed and cut on the diagonal into 5cm lengths

2 tbsp roughly chopped coriander

Salt and freshly ground black pepper

Heat the coconut oil in a wok over a medium heat, add the shallots and cook, stirring frequently, for about 5 minutes until tender but not coloured. Add the garlic, ginger, green chilli, mustard seeds, turmeric, cumin, crushed dried chilli and curry leaves and cook for a further minute.

Pour the coconut milk into the pan, bring to the boil, reduce the heat and simmer for 5 minutes to settle and marry all of the flavours.

Taste the curry sauce and add a little sugar, lime juice, salt and freshly ground black pepper as needed. Tip the beans into the sauce and cook for a further 4–5 minutes until tender. Add the chopped coriander and serve.

PANGRATTATO

Pangrattato is Italian for breadcrumbs and is sometimes referred to as 'poor-man's Parmesan'. Sprinkled on top of pasta it is a perfect vegan sub for Parmesan cheese. It is a brilliant way to use day-old or stale bread and once cooked can be stored in a jar or airtight box for about two weeks. You can also add finely chopped walnuts, hazelnuts or almonds to the mixture, or some chopped thyme, sage or oregano.

MAKES 4–6 SERVINGS

150g sourdough bread,
   crusts removed
½ tsp crushed dried
   chilli flakes
2 tbsp olive oil
½ tsp dried oregano
Salt and freshly ground
   black pepper

Tear the bread into chunks, tip into a food processor with the chilli flakes and whizz into crumbs, retaining some texture. Tip into a mixing bowl, add the olive oil and dried oregano, season well with salt and freshly ground black pepper and mix thoroughly. Tip the crumbs into a large frying pan and cook over a medium heat, stirring frequently until crisp and golden.

SICHUAN STIR-FRIED CELERY

Celery might seem an unlikely candidate for Chinese cooking, but it does feature in some stir-fries. Here it works perfectly — the celery remains crisp and its slight sweetness pairs wonderfully with the hot and sour flavour of Sichuan chilli bean paste. (If you can't find this paste you could use a teaspoon of coarsely ground Sichuan peppercorns instead.)

SERVES 4–6

6–8 celery sticks, trimmed,
  leaves reserved for garnish
1 tbsp sunflower oil
50g unsalted cashews,
  roughly chopped
2 garlic cloves, sliced
3cm piece ginger, julienned
1 small red chilli, deseeded
  and sliced
2 tbsp rice wine or mirin
1 tbsp Sichuan chilli
  bean paste
1 tbsp soy sauce
1 tbsp sesame oil
1 tsp black sesame seeds,
  to serve

Wash the celery, cut each stick into 6cm lengths then each length into 5mm matchsticks. Blanch in a pan of boiling water for 30 seconds and then drain. This will soften its taste and texture.

Heat the sunflower oil in a wok over a medium heat, add the cashews and toast for about 30 seconds, stirring constantly, until golden. Remove from the wok with a slotted spoon and set aside.

Add the garlic, ginger and chilli to the wok and cook, stirring constantly, for about 30 seconds then return the celery and cook for a further 3 minutes or until the celery starts to soften and turn golden at the edges.

Add the rice wine and chilli bean paste, reduce the heat slightly and cook for a further minute. Add the soy sauce and sesame oil, mix to combine and spoon onto a serving plate. Scatter with the toasted cashews, sesame seeds and reserved celery leaves and serve.

QUICK FLATBREADS

*These super-easy flatbreads take moments to prepare. The dough can be resting
while you get on with something else and then cooked just before serving. Change
the seasoning according to your preference, adding chilli powder or flakes, fennel
or cumin seeds, dried fenugreek leaves or chopped fresh coriander to the mixture.*

MAKES 4

250g plain flour, plus extra
  for rolling
½ tsp baking powder
½ tsp salt
½ tsp nigella seeds
½ tsp garlic granules
2 tbsp olive oil
2 tbsp oat or coconut yogurt
125ml water

Tip the flour into a large mixing bowl, add the baking powder, salt, nigella
seeds and garlic granules and whisk together. Make a well in the centre,
add the olive oil, yogurt and water and mix.

Turn out the mixture onto a lightly floured work surface and knead for
1 minute until smooth. Shape into a ball and return the dough to the bowl,
cover and set aside for 30 minutes.

Tip the dough back onto the floured work surface and divide into four
even portions.

Place a large, heavy-based frying pan over a high heat.

Roll each piece of dough into a disc about 22cm diameter and about 2 mm
thick. Cook one flatbread at a time in the hot pan for about 1 minute, without
turning or until it starts to puff up and large air bubbles form on the top and
the underside is pocked with brown spots.

Flip the flatbread over and cook the other side for a further minute until
puffy and covered in golden-brown spots. Keep warm while you cook the
remaining breads.

HANDVO CORN BREAD

MAKES 1 BREAD/SERVES 8

1 large carrot
150g sweetcorn kernels,
  tinned and drained or
  frozen and defrosted
50g young leaf spinach,
  shredded
2–3 tbsp chopped coriander
3 spring onions, trimmed
  and thinly sliced
3 tsp freshly grated ginger
1 large garlic clove, crushed
1 green chilli, finely
  chopped
125g gram flour
125g fine cornmeal
  or polenta
50g rice flour
50g plain flour
1 tsp bicarbonate of soda
1 tsp baking powder
1 tsp nigella seeds
1 tsp caster sugar
½ tsp ground turmeric
½ tsp mild chilli powder
250g dairy-free or coconut
  yogurt
4 tbsp sunflower oil
1 tsp brown mustard seeds
1 tsp cumin seeds
3 tsp sesame seeds
20 fresh curry leaves
1 tsp crushed dried
  chilli flakes
Salt and freshly ground
  black pepper

This dish is an inspired combination of American-style cornbread and Gujarati handvo, a bread where a mix of rice, lentils and split peas is soaked, blended until smooth, and left to ferment overnight before being combined with vegetables and spices then baked. In India it's possible to buy a handvo flour blend but as this is not widely available elsewhere, I've cheated to a greater degree and used what is more widely available. Not only have I adapted the flour but also the spices and technique. You can swap the veggies according to preference and season — peas, spring greens, sliced onions, shredded courgettes and a good handful of fresh fenugreek leaves wouldn't go amiss.

Preheat the oven to 170° fan/190°C/gas mark 5 and oil a 20cm ovenproof frying pan.

Coarsely grate the carrot into a large mixing bowl — you will need 150g. Add the sweetcorn, spinach, coriander, spring onions, ginger, garlic and chilli and mix to combine.

Sift the gram flour, cornmeal, rice flour, plain flour, bicarbonate of soda and baking powder into another large bowl. Add the nigella seeds, sugar, turmeric and chilli powder and season well with salt and freshly ground black pepper.

In a jug whisk together the yogurt, 2 tbsp of the oil and 150ml water. Add to the sifted dry ingredients and mix until smooth. Fold the vegetable mixture into the batter to thoroughly combine. Spoon into the greased frying pan and spread evenly.

In a small frying pan heat the remaining oil over a medium heat. Add the mustard, cumin and sesame seeds, the curry leaves and crushed dried chilli flakes and cook for 30 seconds until the mustard seeds pop. Spoon over the top of the handvo cornbread and bake in the oven for 30 minutes.

Reduce the heat to 140°C fan/160°C/gas mark 3 and cook for a further 10 minutes until the bread is risen and golden brown and a skewer inserted into the middle comes out clean. Leave to cool in the tin for at least 10 minutes then cut into wedges to serve.

FURIKAKE AND VARIATIONS ON A THEME

Furikake is a spicy Japanese seasoning, usually a blend of dried seaweed, sesame seeds, spices and some sort of chilli. A teaspoonful scattered over a bowl of rice, noodles, veggies or soup will enliven even the simplest meal; the uses for and variations of furikake are endless. Here is a selection of furikake that I seem to have on repeat. Add spices and seasoning to suit your tastes — a teaspoon of nutritional yeast, some dried crispy onions, wasabi powder, pistachios, dried herbs… the list goes on. Each recipe will make enough to almost fill 2 jam jars and will keep for at least one month in a cool, dry larder or cupboard.

MAKES ABOUT 2 JARS

KALE AND SEAWEED
50g leafy kale, tough
  stems removed
1 tsp sunflower oil
A good pinch of crushed
  dried chilli flakes
50g sesame seeds
25g sunflower seeds
25g pumpkin seeds
3 sheets of nori
1 tsp sea salt flakes
½ tsp caster sugar

Preheat the oven to 100°C fan/120°C/gas mark ½.

Wash and thoroughly dry the kale, tear the leaves into 8–10cm pieces and toss with the sunflower oil and a seasoning of chilli flakes. Arrange in a single layer on a baking sheet and bake in the oven for about 30 minutes until crisp. Leave the kale to cool and it will crisp further.

Toast the sesame seeds in a dry wok or small frying pan over a low–medium heat for about 1 minute until they just start to turn golden then tip onto the baking tray with the kale. Toast the sunflower and pumpkin seeds in the wok for another minute, stirring frequently until they just start to pop. Leave to cool on the tray with the sesame and kale.

Toast the nori sheets one at a time over a gas flame for 20 seconds until they start to turn from black to dark green and crisp. (If you don't have a gas hob then toast them under the grill for 10–20 seconds.) Crumble the crispy nori into the seed mixture, stir to combine and season with sea salt flakes. Tip the mixture into a food processor and pulse-blend until combined and the kale and nori are finely chopped.

Tip the mixture back onto the tray, taste and add a little more salt or a little sugar if you prefer, leave until cold and then store in screw-top jars at room temperature until ready to use.

VARIATIONS:

MUSHROOM, CHILLI AND SEAWEED

50g sesame seeds

2 sheets of nori

2 tsp dried mushroom powder

2 tsp Korean chilli flakes (gochugaru)

1 tsp garlic granules

1 tsp sea salt flakes

½ tsp sugar

Toast the sesame seeds in a dry frying pan over a medium heat for about 1 minute, stirring frequently, until golden, tip into a food processor and leave to cool slightly. Meanwhile, toast the nori sheets over the gas flame for 20 seconds until crisp. (If you don't have a gas flame toast the nori under the grill for 10–20 seconds or in a moderate oven for 3 minutes.) Crumble the nori into the food processor, add the remaining ingredients and whizz until combined and the nori is finely chopped.

Leave to cool and then store in screw-top jars.

PEANUT, CHILLI AND SESAME

50g redskin peanuts

25g sesame seeds

½ sheet of nori

3 tsp Korean chilli flakes (gochugaru)

1 tsp garlic granules

1 tsp sea salt flakes

1 tsp sugar

Toast the peanuts in a dry frying pan over a medium heat for about 4 minutes, stirring frequently, until golden. Tip into a food processor and leave to cool to room temperature.

Toast the sesame seeds in a dry frying pan over a medium heat for about 1 minute, stirring frequently, until golden. Crisp the nori sheets, following the method in the recipe above. Crumble the nori into the food processor, add the sesame seeds and remaining ingredients and whizz until the nuts are finely chopped and all the ingredients combined.

Leave to cool and then store in screw-top jars.

SEEDS AND SPICE

25g white sesame seeds

25g black sesame seeds

10g poppy seeds

1 tsp dried chilli flakes

½ sheet of nori

1 tsp sea salt flakes

½ tsp freshly ground black pepper

1 tsp garlic granules

1 tsp dried orange peel

1 tsp Korean chilli flakes (gochugaru)

½ tsp sugar

½ tsp ground ginger

Toast the sesame seeds in a dry frying pan over a medium heat for about 1 minute, stirring frequently, until golden. Add the poppy seeds and chilli flakes and cook for another 30 seconds. Tip into a food processor and leave to cool slightly while you toast the nori following the method above.

Crumble the nori into the food processor, add the remaining ingredients and whizz until the nori is finely chopped and the ingredients combined.

Leave to cool and then store in screw-top jars.

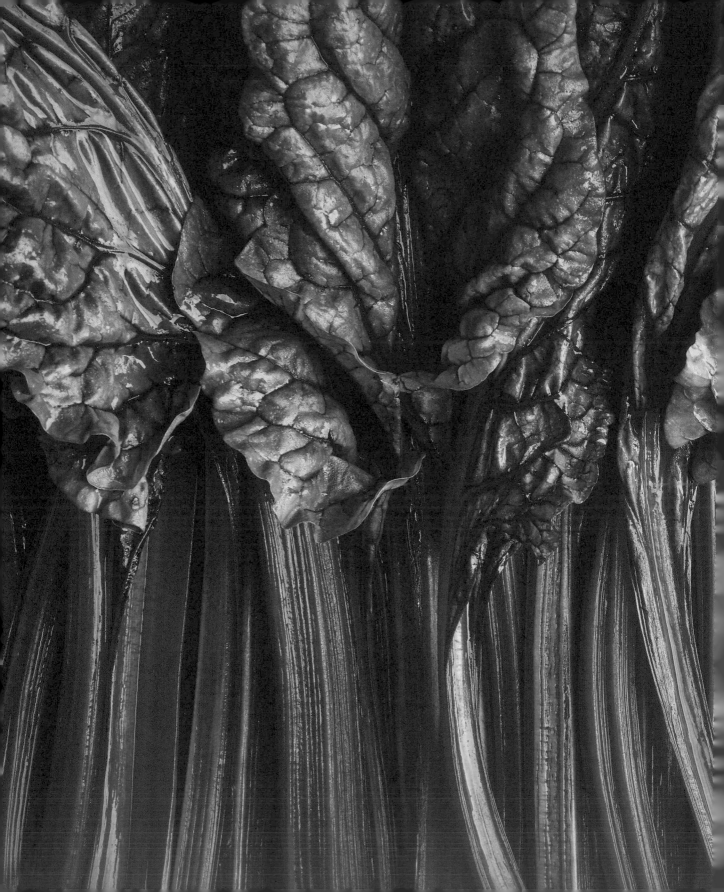

TERMINOLOGY

UK	US
arborio rice	risotto rice
aubergine	eggplant
baking tin	baking pan
baking tray	baking sheet
beansprout	bean sprout
bicarbonate of soda	baking soda
bird's eye chilli	Thai chile (fresh)
butter beans	lima beans
celery stick	celery stalk
chickpeas	garbanzo beans
chilli(es)	chile(s)
Chinese leaf	Chinese cabbage
clingfilm	plastic wrap
coriander	cilantro
cornflour	cornstarch
courgettes	zucchini
easy-blend dried yeast	instant yeast
frying pan	skillet
gram flour	chickpea or besam flour
griddle pan	grill pan
grill	broiler
grill (vb)	broil
kitchen paper	paper towels
Little Gem lettuce	Boston lettuce
mandolin	mandoline
plain flour	all-purpose flour
pine kernels	pine nuts
rapeseed oil	canola oil
runner beans	string beans
self-raising flour	self-rising flour
spring onions	scallions
[small] pak choi	[baby] bok choi
Savoy cabbage	savoy cabbage
spring greens	collard greens
tomato purée	tomato paste

CONVERSION CHART

WEIGHTS

10g	$\frac{1}{4}$oz
15g	$\frac{1}{2}$oz
25g	1oz
30g	1oz
40g	$1\frac{1}{2}$oz
50g	$1\frac{3}{4}$oz
75g	$2\frac{3}{4}$oz
100g	$3\frac{1}{2}$oz
120g	4oz
125g	$4\frac{1}{2}$oz
130g	$4\frac{1}{2}$oz
150g	$5\frac{1}{2}$oz
175g	6oz
180g	$6\frac{1}{3}$oz
200g	7oz
225g	8oz
250g	9oz
270g	$9\frac{1}{2}$oz
300g	$10\frac{1}{2}$oz
350g	12oz
400g	14oz
450g	1lb
500g	1lb 2oz
600g	1 lb 5oz
650g	1 lb 7oz
700g	1lb 9oz
1kg	2lb 3oz

VOLUME

5ml	1 teaspoon	
10ml	1 dessertspoon	
15ml	1 tablespoon	
50ml	$1\frac{3}{4}$fl oz	
75ml	5 tablespoons	
100ml	$3\frac{1}{2}$fl oz	
160ml	$5\frac{1}{2}$fl oz	
175ml	6fl oz	
200ml	7fl oz	
225ml	8fl oz	
250ml	9fl oz	
300ml	$10\frac{1}{2}$fl oz	
350ml	12fl oz	
400ml	14fl oz	
500ml	18fl oz	
700ml	25fl oz	$1\frac{1}{4}$ pints
750ml	26fl oz	
800ml	$27\frac{1}{2}$fl oz	$1\frac{1}{3}$ pints
1 litre	35fl oz	$1\frac{3}{4}$ pints
1.2 litres	$38\frac{1}{2}$fl oz	2 pints
1.4 litres	48fl oz	$2\frac{1}{2}$ pints

LENGTH

2mm	$\frac{3}{32}$in
3mm	$\frac{1}{8}$in
4mm	$\frac{1}{8}$in
5mm	$\frac{1}{4}$in
1cm	$\frac{1}{2}$in
2cm	$\frac{3}{4}$in
3cm	$1\frac{1}{8}$in
4cm	$1\frac{5}{8}$in
5cm	2in
6cm	$2\frac{1}{2}$in
7cm	$2\frac{3}{4}$in
8cm	$3\frac{1}{8}$in
10cm	4in
15cm	6in
20cm	8in
22cm	$8\frac{1}{2}$in
25cm	10in
30cm	12in
40cm	16in

Use either metric or imperial measures, not a mixture of the two.

OVEN TEMPERATURES

DESCRIPTION	FAN	CONVENTIONAL	GAS
Very cool	90°C	110°C/225°F	Gas ¼
Very cool	100°C	120°C/250°F	Gas ½
Cool	120°C	140°C/275°F	Gas 1
Slow	130°C	150°C/300°F	Gas 2
Moderately slow	140°C	160°C/320°F	Gas 3
Moderately slow	150°C	170°C/325°F	Gas 3
Moderate	160°C	180°C/360°F	Gas 4
Moderately hot	170°C	190°C/375°F	Gas 5
Hot	180°C	200°C/400°F	Gas 6
Very hot	200°C	220°C/425°F	Gas 7
Very hot	210°C	230°C/450°F	Gas 8
Hottest	220°C	240°C/475°F	Gas 9

INDEX

ACKNOWLEDGEMENTS

I like to say a huge thank you to the amazing team involved in the making of this beautiful book.

To the fabulous team at Pavilion — to Lucy Smith for starting the ball rolling and then to Clare Double for taking up the reins. Both of you are a joy to work with. To Laura Russell and Kei Ishimaru for your beautiful design and to Katie Hewett for your eagle-eyed proofreading and Hilary Bird for indexing.

To Nassima Rothacker — any time spent with Nass is uplifting and filled with laughter. I love days spent with her making beautiful pictures and she's done me proud again with the stunning photographs in this book.

To my wonderful assistants — Lola Milne and Sarah Vassallo — thank you both for keeping the wheels rolling in the kitchen on some fast-paced but fun cooking days.

And to Hughie for being the best taste tester and voice of reason.